3 | *Short Topics in*
System Administration

System Security:
A Management Perspective

David L. Oppenheimer, David A. Wagner, and Michele D. Crabb

Edited by Dan Geer

Published by the USENIX Association for
SAGE, the System Administrators Guild
1997

Copies of these publications are available to members of SAGE for $5.00
and to non-members for $7.50. Outside the USA and Canada, please
add $3.50 per copy for postage (via printed matter).

For copies and for membership information, please contact:

The USENIX Association
2560 Ninth Street, Suite 215
Berkeley, CA 94107 USA
Telephone: 510.528.8649
Email: *office @ usenix.org*
Web: *http://www.usenix.org*

First Printing, March 1997
Second Printing, September 1997
Third Printing, July 1998

Many of the designations used by manufacturers and sellers to distinguish their products are claimed as trademarks. Where those designations appear in this publication, and USENIX was aware of a trademark
claim, the designations have been printed in caps or initial caps.

Printed in the United States of America, on 50% recycled paper, 10-15%
post-consumer waste.

Acknowledgments

The authors offer their sincere appreciation to Barb Dijker and Dan Geer for their many helpful suggestions.

Contents

 # Foreword

Security is a goal, a state of nature to aspire to. Security technology and security practice are means, not ends. The apparent tension between these two claims is what this booklet is about. It is what an educated consumer of security claims needs to understand.

Clearly, something big is happening in the world of information technology (IT). This booklet is aimed at IT management, specifically, the part of IT management where computing seems less well definable with every passing day. As of now, your business so thoroughly runs on information it would die hard without IT. The computing you do is increasingly volatile, a mix of Internet and intranet for which the margin for error seems ever thinner.

Outsiders know this, and they probe you. Insiders know this, and they evade you. Yet never before has security technology so truly been an enabling technology. With the right security, the global marketplace is waiting. With the right security, you can use the Web for a fresh round of automation that puts real dollars on the bottom line by making your information work for you at much lower costs. With the right security, you are more free, not more boxed in.

Security is, more than anything else, a way of thinking. You need to know how to think the "security way" if you want to know when to use what tool or how to sagely evaluate the claims of vendors. You need to think clearly about security if you are to "keep your head when those about you are losing theirs and blaming it on you." You need to be able to teach others if you are to use security to leapfrog your most serious competition, viz., ignorance and inertia.

We hope you'll read this booklet with a mindset about what can be. We will have succeeded if we have done nothing more than whet your appetite.

Dan Geer
January 1997

1.0 Introduction

Information is at the heart of almost every modern business. Manufacturers keep records of vendors, customers, and financial accounts. Educational institutions maintain data about purchasing, fee payments, and students' academic records, and they often provide information systems (e.g., computer workstations, fileservers, and networks) for use by their students. Government agencies, and some private companies with government clients, may process sensitive or classified information. Indeed, in today's "information economy," the end product of many organizations *is* information. Because information is vital to almost all organizations, the livelihood of almost everyone employed in business, education, or government depends on the quality and integrity of business information—information that is increasingly stored on computers.

Unfortunately, as organizations have become more reliant on computerized information, the computer systems they use have become increasingly vulnerable. Companies that formerly used desktop computers hardwired to mainframe systems now possess extensive internal Local Area Networks (LANs) and external network connections via the Internet, ISDN lines, and modem dialup. Attracted by the promise of intraoffice and worldwide electronic mail, access to Internet resources, and the ability to advertise and sell their services via the World Wide Web, companies are rushing to access the "information superhighway"—often without considering the associated risks. Further aggravating the current security problem is the fact that the most popular and cost-effective computing model has shifted from one that is mainframe based to one in which computing power, and hence critical business resources, are distributed throughout a network that can span a building, a corporate campus, or even the globe. This proliferation and distribution of resources means that organizations have opened their computing environments, and hence their lifeblood, to an unprecedented—and, unfortunately, often unappreciated—level of risk.

This rush by organizations to stay on the leading edge of computer technology has led to rapid growth in the number of computer security violations and the costs associated with security incidents. The Computer Emergency Response Team (CERT), a federally funded computer security incident clearinghouse at Carnegie Mellon University, has documented an increase in the number of incidents reported each year since the organization's inception in 1989. These statistics are even more alarming given that much—some say most—computer crime is never reported.

Your data, communications, and reputation are at stake. If you currently store sensitive or critical data on your computers, you are taking a risk. If your business model depends on the reliability and availability of your computers, the success of your business is at risk. If you use email or other forms of electronic communication in your daily work, that too is at risk. Yet the highest stakes may be the reputation of your organization. Security is a hot issue, and recent episodes of system penetrations have received prominent coverage in many newspapers and television news reports. Some large corporations are discovering that loss of public confidence and the public relations nightmares that follow a highly publicized security compromise can significantly outstrip the monetary damage done to the corporate computing resources. Even if *your* business does not store critical data online, protecting your company's reputation may be reason enough for concern.

Without question, organizations stand to gain much from increased use of computers and access to worldwide computer networks and resources. But it is extremely unwise to venture into these uncharted technological territories without understanding the risks, formulating a security policy, and making adequate provisions for protecting your important business data. This booklet provides a nontechnical overview of computer security issues for information systems managers and executives who must make decisions that affect their organization's security infrastructure.

Implementing computer security can be a "chicken and egg" process in terms of deciding where to start. On the one hand, you must first understand what threats exist and how you can reduce your vulnerability. On the other hand, you must also be aware of what assets you want to protect, what value those assets possess, and what level of security is appropriate given the culture and philosophy of your organization.

We begin with a discussion of common threats to computer systems and possible responses. In this discussion, we look at hardware threats (e.g., natural disasters), methods of authentication, threats to software and data, and the importance of educating users and support staff about the dangers of social engineering attacks. We then turn to a discussion of policy issues, including striking a balance between protection and expense, performing a risk analysis, selecting an appropriate trust model, defining a security policy, planning for and recovering from contingencies, and implementing your security policy in a way that provides genuine and continued protection. Our emphasis in this section is on technical and procedural aspects of implementing security policies; for a detailed discussion of writing policy documents, we refer you to *A Guide to Developing Computing Policy Documents,* edited by Barbara L. Dijker (USENIX Association, 1996). We conclude with a discussion of how you can put to work the information contained in this booklet and how you can ensure that your security controls continue to function as expected in the future.

We have provided two appendices containing related information. Appendix A discusses what we feel are the top ten computer security problems that plague organizations, and Appendix B lists a number of useful computer security resources.

Before embarking on a detailed discussion of security issues, we want to emphasize that security is all about trade-offs. The only truly secure computer system is the one that is never plugged into an electric outlet. Your organization must therefore select the level of security it considers appropriate by weighing the potential impact and likelihood of a security incident against the cost and effect on worker productivity of potential protective measures. Many risks can be avoided with inexpensive and unobtrusive security controls. Other risks require more elaborate protection. In this booklet, we hope to make clear which risks and responses fall into each category, enabling you to decide on an appropriate security infrastructure for your organization.

Computer Security Threats and Responses

Responses	Environmental Threats	Power Failure	Physical Attack	Accidental Physical Damage	Tempest	Network Snooper	Active Network Attack	Undesired System Access	Social Enginee
Environmental controls	PMDR								
Environmental alarms (temperature, humidity, fire, smoke, water)	D								
Surge Suppression	PM								
Uninterruptible power supply		PMDR							
Physical protection of equipment	PM		PMD	PM	M			P (on-site attack)	
Physical protection of network	PM		PMD	PM	M			P (on-site attack)	
Redundancy in network	MR		MR	MR					
Software-based one-time passwords								P	
Hardware-based one-time passwords								P	
Biometric authentication								P	
Backups	R		R	R				MR	
RAID	MR			MR					
Cryptography for secrecy						P			
Cryptography for integrity authentication							P	P	
Audit logs								D	
Firewall								PD	
User education				PM					PMDR
Backup site for data processing	MR		MR	MR					
Use of TPEP-evaluated equipment (see chapter 6)								PMD	

Key: P=prevent; M=mitigate; D=detect; R=recover

This table outlines several major categories of computer security threats and some possible responses to them. The responses are categorized as helping to prevent or mitigate the threat, or detect or recover from an incident stemming from the threat. These threats and responses are discussed in section 2.0.

2.0 Threats and Responses

We begin our discussion of computer system security with a close examination of the most common threats and the possible responses to them. Though the nature of these threats varies from attacks on hardware to attacks on software and data, the goals of an attack can generally be categorized as: causing unauthorized disclosure of information (failure of confidentiality); unauthorized modification of information (integrity failure); or denial of service (failure of availability).

Throughout this chapter we will mention uses of *cryptography*. Cryptography is the study of *encryption* and *decryption*. For the purposes of our discussion, encryption is the encoding of a message so that it can be read only by authorized individuals, and decryption is the process of decoding an encrypted message. In *symmetric key cryptography* a message (called *plaintext*) is encoded using a secret *key* shared by the sender and receiver. The receiver uses this key to decode the encrypted message (called *ciphertext* while it is in its encoded form), recovering the original plaintext. Cryptographic systems are designed so that it is impossible for a person to transform the ciphertext into plaintext (i.e., decode the message) without knowing the key. *Public key cryptography*, an alternative to symmetric key cryptography, is described in section 2.3.3.2.

2.1 Hardware Threats and Responses

Hardware security is the oldest area of computer security; it predates multiuser systems, computer communication networks, and widespread public access to computer equipment. The threats to computer hardware have not changed significantly since the time of mainframes housed behind glass windows, though some risks have increased in this age of distributed computing when critical hardware is often spread throughout an organization's entire campus. For maximum reliability and security, hardware should be protected against threats from the natural environment, electrical fluctuations, unwanted human manipulation, and undesired electromagnetic emanations. No protection scheme is perfect—even the most comprehensive precautions can fail. Thorough and regular backups, stored both on- and offsite, offer the most realistic last line of defense in the event of hardware damage or malfunction. Backups are discussed in section 2.3.1.1.

2.1.1 *Natural Disasters* Although natural disasters such as violent weather, fire, and earthquakes cannot be prevented, measures can be taken to minimize their impact. Because many of these forces can damage noncomputer equipment, you may already be equipped with adequate protection against some of these dangers. But computers are more sensitive than most other electronic equipment to variations in their environment, and as a result, special precautions should be taken to protect them against these contingencies.

- Temperature/humidity: Computers can be damaged by extremes in temperature or humidity. These conditions may result from violent weather or from a breakdown of environmental control equipment such as air conditioning. Computers are usually shipped with printed information specifying the temperature range within which the equipment can be safely operated. Computers should be kept in temperature- and humidity-controlled rooms, and alarms should be installed in those rooms to notify the appropriate personnel if the safe range of either is exceeded.

- Fire: A modern business facility is almost certainly already protected by smoke detectors, but special precautions should be taken to protect computer equipment from fire and smoke. This means extra smoke detectors, frequent testing of detectors, fire extinguishers throughout the facility, and adequate means to notify appropriate personnel in case fire or smoke is detected. You may wish to use gas-based fire extinguishing equipment such as halon or carbon dioxide rather than water sprinklers because these gases will not damage computer equipment if they are released during a fire. Water almost certainly will cause damage.

- Water: Damaging water can come not only from violent weather, but also from plumbing problems or from intentional or accidental release of water from fire sprinkler systems. The best protection against water damage is installation of water sensors throughout the areas populated by computers; a particularly good location is underneath the raised floors commonly found in computer rooms. These sensors can notify appropriate personnel at the first sign of water accumulation. A rapid response can prevent a minor situation from turning into a major disaster. The danger from storm water accumulation can also be minimized by locating computer rooms at or above the second floor of a building.

- Earthquakes and other strong vibrations: Although not all areas of the world are prone to earthquakes, strong vibrations can arise from many sources, such as construction work, aircraft, or large vehicles passing near a building. You can minimize the chance that strong vibration will damage your equipment by keeping equipment securely on a floor or on sturdy furniture and away from windows and other structures that might break during a strong vibration. Also take into account what you have placed near or above computer equipment, because it might fall on top of that equipment as the result of a strong vibration.

2.1.2 *Electrical Problems* Electrical problems take many forms, and all are potentially devastating to computer equipment. These problems include power surges, blackouts, brownouts, and static electricity. All sensitive electronic equipment should be protected from power surges by the use of surge protectors. But important equipment, including compute servers, fileservers, and networking equipment, should be powered by an uninterruptible power supply (UPS). A UPS will protect equipment not only from power surges but also from brownouts and blackouts. The cost of a UPS unit varies with the amount and duration of the backup power it can supply. A UPS is particularly valuable when used in conjunction with special software that warns logged-in users of a power failure and shuts down equipment safely upon detecting a power outage. In this case, only a few minutes of backup power can provide users with enough time to save their work and can provide the computer's operating system an opportunity to shut down the machine so that files are not corrupted. Current UPSs cost about 40 cents per watt for a unit that will provide about five minutes of backup power.

If your organization is located in an area prone to lengthy power outages or your organization's work must continue even in the face of power outages, you stand to benefit from a second level of power protection, e.g., a gasoline generator. Assuming your battery-based UPS can power your equipment until the gasoline generator is activated, this combination ensures a continuous, uninterrupted supply of power.

Static electricity, the second type of electrical problem we discuss, poses a serious threat to computer equipment. In order to avoid damaging sensitive electrical parts, ground yourself to a good electrical ground using a wrist strap or similar device before touching the internal components of a computer or its peripherals. Consider installing antistatic carpeting in rooms used to work on computer hardware.

2.1.3 *Human Threats: Restricting Physical Access to Computer Systems* In the current age of distributed computing, the technical need for a central "computer center" or "computer room" is diminishing. But there remains at least one strong argument in favor of concentrating computer equipment in one or a small number of locations: physical security. It is far easier to protect a single room or a floor of a building than to protect an entire corporate campus and the homes of telecommuting employees. At the very least, keep major servers, networking equipment, and backup media as well protected physically as your organization's financial resources allow.

Physical access to sensitive computer areas and the equipment within them can be controlled through a number of low-tech and high-tech measures. The former category includes door locks and equipment locks (the latter lock computer equipment to a very heavy object such as a desk). The value of equipment locks is questionable, however: they do nothing to prevent unauthorized use of the locked equipment, and they often do not prevent removal of components from the locked equipment (e.g., removal of internal disk drives, memory chips, peripheral boards, etc. from a computer). At best, they may be useful as a deterrent to the casual thief.

Another caveat related to traditional physical locks applies to door locks. Door locks are useless if the wall in which the door is placed stops at a dropped ceiling; the intruder can probably climb over the wall without difficulty. Door locks are also of no value when placed on a door with its hinges on the outside of the protected room; an intruder can simply remove the hinges and then the door. Though often overlooked during building design, these types of vulnerabilities are easily observed by those with access to the building and hence can enable burglary by "insiders."

The high-tech devices for enforcing security fall into two main categories: alarms and locks. Alarms range from simple hardwired systems that sense when a door or window has been opened to elaborate systems with motion detectors, floor pressure sensors, glass-break detectors, closed-circuit television, and the like. Locks can also be simple or complex. Two types of sophisticated "locks" are becoming popular, so we discuss them briefly here.

Locks based on "smart cards" similar to automatic teller machine cards are a popular physical access control mechanism. Unlike regular keys, these systems require both "something you have" (the card) and "something you know" (usually a secret personal identification number [PIN]). It is theoretically infeasible to obtain the PIN by simply examining the card; this can be implemented by storing the PIN in a computer with which the lock communicates for PIN verification or by encrypting the PIN and storing it on the card in encrypted form.

For the highest security applications, locks based on biometrics are becoming increasingly popular. Although some of these systems are quite expensive, they go the farthest in ensuring that the individual physically present at the lock is actually the person he or she claims to be. Biometric devices operate by examining one or more physical or behavioral characteristics of an individual. Among the characteristics used by advanced locks are fingerprints, voiceprints, typing pattern, and handwriting pattern. If measured sensitively enough, any of these characteristics, when compared to the corresponding measurements of the authorized individual, can provide a great deal of assurance that the individual identifying him or herself to the lock is authorized to open it. Handprint locks are one of the least expensive types of biometric locks; they are available for about $1,000.

2.1.4 Network and Communication Vulnerabilities
In section 2.4, we discuss technical vulnerabilities of computer networks, and in section 5.1, we present some policies that can help to minimize those vulnerabilities. Here we briefly discuss two physical threats to your network infrastructure: unauthorized access and network failure. Though we are primarily concerned with computer data communication networks, the comments in this section apply equally to telephone communication networks.

Modern computer networks are built primarily from physical cables. Intruders who gain access to these cables can monitor all data that passes along them and can even inject their own data into the stream of network traffic. In response to this threat, organizations with serious security concerns may choose to route network wires through pressurized conduit. If an attacker attempts to break into the conduit, the pressure inside the conduit will change. An alarm is installed within the conduit to notify appropriate security personnel when such a change in pressure occurs.

Because network wiring is vulnerable to physical attack, all organizations should think carefully about where they install new wiring. Cables should stay behind walls or under floors whenever possible. Wiring closets should remain locked at all times, and networking equipment should be protected with the same care as is sensitive computer equipment.

Although protecting the physical integrity of the computer network within your organization may be difficult, protecting the integrity of wide-scale public external networks such as the Internet is inconceivable. In section 2.4, we discuss the risks inherent in connecting to a public network, and we present some technical measures that can be taken to mitigate those risks.

Failure of your organization's network may result from any of the threats discussed in the previous three sections. Whether a failure arises from human attack or technical problems, the best protection is redundancy. If your organization would be devastated by a loss of Internet connectivity, consider acquiring network service from two or more Internet providers. You can choose for all but one to serve as "backup" providers in case the primary provider fails. You may wish to establish multiple redundant lines from your organization to your network provider, particularly if you use only one network provider. And though it may seem obvious, many organizations have overlooked the necessity of physically separating backup cables from one another. If one cable serves as the primary connection to your Internet provider and three others serve as backup, route them out of four different corners of your facility. That way the next individual who starts digging on or near your site is unlikely to destroy all of your primary and backup cables in one fell swoop.

One often overlooked aspect of backup network service is network routing outside your facility. Backup connections purchased from a single provider are likely to route traffic identically once the data have left the area served by that provider. Even backup connections purchased from different providers may join and follow a single path upon leaving your geographic region. If 24-hour network connectivity is essential to your business, ask your provider(s) for "diverse routing" for your backup connections—in other words, make sure the backups travel different routes to the Internet backbone networks. Unfortunately, this goal is much more difficult to achieve, and its implications for connectivity are much more serious, than it might at first appear. As an example, much of the state of Minnesota was cut off from the Internet for over 12 hours on September 15, 1996, because of technical problems experienced by a single network provider (Lee, Theodore M. P., *RISKS Digest*, vol. 18, no. 46).

Redundancy can also be employed within your organization's internal network. Though it is costly (and in some cases impossible) to equip every network device with two network interfaces, some models of some network equipment, such as hubs, routers, and switches, offer redundancy features that can provide backup connections between network segments.

The security of wireless networks and wireless portions of mostly wired networks is beyond the scope of this booklet. You should be aware, however, that it is a simple matter to eavesdrop on many forms of wireless communication. Encryption of such transmissions is essential to ensuring privacy. Encryption is also an essential technique for maintaining data privacy and integrity in wired networks. We discuss cryptographic protection of network traffic in section 2.4.

2.1.5 EMFs and TEMPEST In this booklet, we suggest dozens of techniques you can use to protect yourself against individuals wishing to access your organization's information without authorization. But one threat we haven't yet discussed is perhaps the most difficult human threat to protect against because an intruder's use of it is undetectable. This vulnerability arises from the electromagnetic radiation (often called EMFs, an abbreviation for Electro-Magnetic Frequencies) emitted by all electronic devices. Unfortunately, among these devices are video display terminals (e.g., computer screens) and network cables. With a few hundred dollars' worth of equipment, it is now possible to monitor emissions from video display equipment and to reconstruct the original signal—in effect, allowing anyone to read your computer display screen from up to hundreds of feet away. Monitoring emissions from cables is generally considered to be more difficult than monitoring video display emissions.

You can protect against electronic eavesdropping, but it's almost impossible to eliminate the EMF monitoring risk altogether. The commonly used protection techniques include isolation, shielding, and source suppression.

Isolation relies on the fact that the difficulty of detecting and isolating the electromagnetic signals emitted by electronic equipment increases with the receiver's distance from the source of those signals. Put another way, it is far safer to keep sensitive computer equipment in the middle of a building at the center of a highly guarded corporate campus than to place your computer terminal on a desk facing a storefront window along a busy street.

Protection by *shielding* derives from the fact that electromagnetic signals cannot escape a hollow metal conductor (e.g., a hollow cube of copper). A piece of equipment can be shielded, or an entire room or building can be protected, by encapsulating the protected area in such a metal. Unfortunately, this sort of protection can be very expensive. A related, less expensive, but less effective technique is to attach a fine metallic mesh to the front of computer screens you wish to protect.

Finally, *source suppression* refers to designing electronic components so that the EMF signals they emit are not strong enough (or not correlated enough to the data passing through the equipment) to permit EMF-based eavesdropping. Unfortunately, this technology must generally be built into the device when it is manufactured, and commodity computer parts are not built with TEMPEST protection in mind.

Naturally, the United States government is very interested in protecting its computer equipment from eavesdroppers. The term *TEMPEST,* which has come to describe the threat from electronic eavesdropping of the form we've been discussing, originated with the US Government. Unfortunately, government documents related to protecting against the threat are classified. In fact, the government will not even explain the meaning of the term TEMPEST.

In general, isolation is the only cost-effective approach for most organizations to protect against the TEMPEST threat. Because existing nonmilitary TEMPEST eavesdropping devices appear to have a rather limited distance range, a reasonable way to protect against TEMPEST is to establish a good physical security perimeter around buildings that house sensitive data-processing and communication equipment.

2.2 Authenticating People

An important facet of system security is *authentication*, the process by which individuals prove their identity to a system. Authentication is vital to security for several reasons. First, legitimate parties need to be able to prove to the system that they deserve access, and the system needs to be able to stop illegitimate entities from gaining access. Second, the system frequently needs to be able to distinguish among those users who are permitted to access the system; for example, one group of users may have permission to read a certain file, but others may not. Finally, many systems keep audit logs of significant actions taken by users (see section 2.3.4). The system must possess accurate information about who is performing an action in order to generate a valid log entry.

The strength of the authentication technology you deploy must match the level of protection required by your security needs. There are many choices in the area of authentication devices. As with all security decisions, ease of use and level of assurance provided must be balanced against cost and inconvenience to users.

User authentication methods are usually divided into three basic approaches, which can be summarized as authentication based on "something you know," "something you have," or "something you are." Requiring a secret password is an example of authentication based on "something you know." Schemes based on possession of a hardware token or magnetic-striped card are typical of "something you have" security technology. Finally, biometric methods such as retinal scanning or fingerprint verification are examples of authentication based on "something you are."

2.2.1 Threats Typical computer usage can be divided into three scenarios: users physically present at the computer system to which they are authenticating themselves, remote authentication over a LAN, and remote authentication across the Internet or another open, untrusted network. Each scenario carries with it different vulnerabilities.

Authentication of an individual who is physically present at a computer system typically requires only simple techniques, under the assumption that the room or building where the system is located has strong physical protection against unauthorized access. In this case, a simple password system is generally sufficient.

When an adversary has access to (or control over) a network to which the target system is connected (this is typically the case for machines connected to the Internet), the situation becomes much more dangerous, and simple passwords are insufficient. In a *passive attack*, the adversary eavesdrops on the network and can watch the contents of data packets sent over it. In particular, any passwords sent on the network segment being monitored can be captured and later used by attackers to authenticate themselves to the system. Monitoring of passwords passing through a network is often known as *password sniffing*, and attackers are said to *replay* an authentication session when they use the password data they captured in order to later gain access to the system. Protection against this attack requires a "one-time password" system, which we describe in section 2.2.4.

In an *active attack*, the attacker can actually modify the contents of the network packets at will. Active attacks are more dangerous than passive attacks because they allow an attacker to modify data sent during, or to completely take over, an already authenticated network connection. Protection against this attack requires that each data packet be individually authenticated by the machine to which it is sent. Such protection is not standard in modern networks such as Ethernet and the Internet, but it can be added with special hardware or software. Per-packet authentication is part of the new Internet standard, IPv6, which is expected to see widespread use by the year 2000.

2.2.2 No Authentication   One possible authentication policy is to require no authentication. For example, the MS-DOS, Microsoft Windows 3.x and 95, and Macintosh operating systems do not require users to authenticate themselves if they are physically present at the computer. This may be sufficient for a single-user, standalone workstation in a room or building with strong physical security: the physical locks control all access, so software controls may not be necessary. But this approach is not reasonable for a machine that contains sensitive data or that can be physically accessed by untrusted individuals.

2.2.3 Reusable Passwords: Something You Know   The most common form of user authentication is reusable password: to be granted access, users must supply their secret password when they login to the system; the password they use does not change between login sessions, unless they explicitly change it (hence the term "reusable" to describe this password system). Reusable password protection is a simple, cheap, and widespread method for authentication; however, there are several serious limitations associated with the security of such passwords. Even if you do not intend to use reusable password authentication, you should understand its limitations because more sophisticated authentication technologies have been developed largely to address the numerous weaknesses of reusable passwords.

Reusable passwords are subject to guessing attacks. In most systems, users are allowed to pick their own passwords, and untrained users often select easily guessed passwords. All too often users will simply enter their username, last name, pet's name, birthdate, a swear word, or another easily guessed phrase when asked to select a password. Also, many systems come with default passwords established for certain standard system maintenance accounts. Intruders know about these default passwords, and they have also developed many tools to automate trial-and-error guessing of user-selected passwords. Password guessing is an extremely widespread method of system penetration, and malicious hackers have been actively taking advantage of weak passwords for many years. For example, the Internet worm which infected many sites on the Internet in 1988 automated password-guessing by trying the following:

no password

username

username repeated twice

user's first name

user's last name

username written backwards

an internal list of 432 "likely" passwords

the online system dictionary, with capitalized words spelled also in lower case

(Don Seeley. "A Tour of the Worm." University of Utah Computer Science Department Technical Report UUCS-89-009, 1989)

An alternative to allowing users to select their own reusable passwords is to have the system choose random, "difficult-to-guess" passwords and to force users to employ them. Unfortunately, these difficult-to-guess passwords are also generally difficult to remember, and users often respond by writing them down (picture a yellow Post-it note stuck to the monitor), thus eliminating the purpose of the password. To be effective, passwords should not be written down anywhere.

Yet another pitfall associated with reusable passwords is the threat of password sniffing, described in section 2.2.1. An adversary with access to the network wire can readily snoop on a connection, capture the password, and then reuse it to gain access to the system. Software for password sniffing has been readily available in the malicious hacker community for several years, and the frequency of password sniffing is on the rise. To avoid this problem, don't use reusable passwords, especially for privileged system accounts.

Finally, there is one more risk associated with using passwords for authentication across untrusted networks. Password authentication only proves the user's identity initially at login time; subsequent data packets associated with that connection can be modified by a malicious attacker. Recent attacks have gone as far as allowing the attacker to completely "hijack" a session, putting the attacker in control of all packets that appear to come from the already authenticated user. The theory behind such active attacks is readily available, but fortunately, the implementation requires some sophistication and knowledge. Accordingly, the incidence of connection hijacking seems to be relatively low at present, and tools to undertake this attack do not appear to be widely available in the hacker community—yet. It is worth noting, however, that we are aware of at least two commercial programs that will perform connection hijacking. In short, although active attacks are currently rare, they are a threat to high-security environments and are likely to become more prevalent in the future.

In summary, reusable password authentication has serious limitations. The future of reusable passwords for authentication across open networks looks short. However, reusable passwords are simple and widespread, so they may be adequate for very low security environments.

If reusable passwords are deemed sufficient, users should be urged to choose phrases that are difficult to guess. For example, the passwords should include a mixture of uppercase, lowercase, numeric, and nonalphanumeric characters. Software for UNIX systems that will prevent users from choosing "easily guessed" passwords is publicly available; with some of these programs, the system administrator can set the rules as to what defines an "easy-to-guess" password. Reusable passwords should be changed frequently enough to reduce the risk that they will have been guessed by an attacker or monitored during a network login, but infrequently enough so that users are encouraged to select difficult-to-guess (and hence, unfortunately, difficult-to-remember) passwords. Many operating systems allow system administrators to set a maximum "lifetime" for passwords; after passwords expire, users are automatically prompted to select new ones the next time they login to the system.

2.2.4 One-time Passwords In an attempt to address the security vulnerabilities of reusable passwords, some sites use "one-time password" systems. These systems still involve sending a password over a network, but each password can be used for only one login. A simple one-time password system would involve loading a computer system with several hundred passwords for each user and then giving users a list of their personal passwords. Each time users wished to login, they would type in the next password on their list and then cross it off.

Clearly, there are some serious problems with this one-time password system: the user must carry a huge list of passwords, and the system must somehow store a separate list of passwords for each user.

Both of these problems can be addressed as follows. The computer stores a single secret password for each user; this password is only known to the system and that user. When the user wishes to login, the computer asks for the username and then presents the user with a random number. The user uses the secret password to encrypt the random number and sends back the reply. (Users could in principle perform this encryption by hand if they were extremely fast at performing mathematical computations, but in practice, they would be more likely to use a trusted computer and program to perform the encryption. The device performing the encryption must be trusted because users are typing into it their single, secret password.) At the same time, the computer encrypts the random number it generated using the secret password it has stored for the user. If this result matches what the user enters, the user is granted access. If we imagine that the random numbers are so random as to never be used more than once per user, and that the results of the encryption follow no discernible pattern, then this is a one-time password scheme. This is clearly better than the list-based one-time password scheme: the user has to remember only one password, and the computer has to store only one password per user; yet an attacker monitoring the network is still foiled in any attempt to benefit from password sniffing.

One-time password schemes similar to the one just described are currently employed by many organizations. Software supporting one-time passwords is publicly available for UNIX systems; an example is the program S/Key. Although one-time passwords do not resist session hijacking (because they authenticate only the initial login and not subsequent communication), they do resist the more common form of network attack: password sniffing. The drawback to this system is that the user must trust the computer performing the encryption not to disclose, store, or otherwise misuse the secret password. In the next section, we describe a way to generate one-time passwords in a secure way, essentially by providing users with their own very small, trusted computer.

2.2.5 Hardware Tokens: Something You Have

In contrast to passwords, hardware tokens allow authentication based on "something you have." Individuals authorized to access a system are issued a small physical device that is unique to each user; to login, the user must have the hardware device in hand. Because each token is user-specific, the system can identify individuals uniquely based on the information that the token provides.

A hardware token system could involve simply sliding a credit card-type card through a reader attached to a computer system, but the more common use of hardware tokens is as part of a one-time password system (generally implemented as a "challenge-response" system). At login time, the system issues a random one-time *challenge* that is entered into the handheld authenticator. The token then computes the appropriate *response*, and the user types that value as the password. The computer system verifies the response by performing the same operation on the challenge as did the authenticator that it knows the user should possess. Note that in this case, the user need not remember any password, but if the authenticator is stolen, the thief can masquerade as the authorized user without being detected. (We will see shortly how this drawback can be addressed.)

Time-based hardware tokens are a slight twist on the previously described system. Challenge-response tokens require users to enter a system-supplied challenge into their token, and some users complain that this is inconvenient. Time-based tokens eliminate the need to enter challenges into the token. A time-based hardware token displays on its screen an ever-changing value that the user supplies to the system as the password. Another way to think of a time-based token is as a device that uses the current time as an implicit challenge and computes a response from it, much as challenge-response tokens do. Therefore, the token and the computer system performing the authentication must remain time-synchronized, or at least the authentication computer must be able to compute the token's view of the "current time" given its own view of the "current time." This latter task is not as difficult as it sounds because clock inaccuracy can generally be approximated by a single, measurable number, e.g., "the clock on this card gains one second every year relative to an atomic clock" or "the clock on this card loses five seconds every month relative to an atomic clock."

To prevent compromise in the case of theft, many tokens require the user to enter a short PIN to activate the token. This can be thought of as adding "something you know" authentication to the "something you have" token device, and it combines the advantages of both approaches. The PIN makes the token useless to a thief if the token is stolen.

The largest disadvantage of hardware tokens is their cost, in terms of initial investment for the hardware, deployment of the devices to each user, and replacement, administration, and maintenance. When a software-based password is forgotten, a system administrator can simply set a new password for the user. But when a handheld authenticator is lost or damaged, new hardware must be purchased. In general, hardware tokens tend to impose a large administrative cost above and beyond the cost of the tokens themselves. Another disadvantage of hardware tokens is that the algorithms they use to generate their responses are often proprietary; such algorithms are more likely to be faulty (and therefore insecure) than software-based algorithms that have been subjected to public scrutiny.

Although software-based, one-time password systems of the type described in section 2.2.4 are probably the least expensive type of practical one-time password system to use, a system's entire security is compromised if a user decides to compute a response to the system's challenge using an untrusted computer. Hardware tokens are in essence small, trusted computers that compute the response securely and thus guarantee that the user will employ a trusted, secure mechanism to compute the response.

In the end, managers and security experts will have to decide whether the increased security provided by hardware tokens is worth the extra cost. Our view is that although tokens are probably not worth the expense and hassle of deployment to an organization's entire user base, they can be a wise investment if they are given to employees who frequently access the organization's internal computers remotely from external networks (e.g., the Internet) or who access privileged system accounts remotely from internal or external networks.

2.2.6 Biometric Approaches: Something You Are Biometric approaches attempt to authenticate users by analyzing unforgeable biological patterns: "something you are." Some examples of actual and proposed biometric schemes are fingerprinting, retinal scans, voiceprint analysis, recognition of handwritten signatures, and analysis of typing patterns (especially interkeystroke delays). Even lipprints have been suggested. Biometric authentication is typically associated with extremely high levels of security, such as what the military might use. But although biometric techniques currently require special and often expensive hardware to perform authentication, it is only a matter of time before the costs for such equipment decrease and use of biometric authentication becomes more widespread.

2.3 Protecting Software and Data

Authenticating people is a large piece of the security puzzle, but computer security also has as a prime concern the protection of online information and software against tampering, disclosure, and loss of availability resulting from compromise of system components other than the authentication mechanism.

2.3.1 Availability: Backups and RAIDs The standard approach to providing high availability of a service is to replicate it. By duplicating hardware and software resources, an organization can ensure that backup data and processing power are always standing by in the event of a hardware or software failure. In this section, we discuss two types of replication: backups and RAID (redundant array of inexpensive disks). A third type of replication, the "cold site" or "hot site" backup data-processing center that can be used in the event of a disaster, is discussed in section 5.6.

2.3.1.1 Backups The best way to ensure a speedy recovery from disk failure, accidental deletion of data or programs, or intentional malicious deletion of data or programs is to make frequent backups of your important data. Certainly, this includes the data stored on your fileservers, but in a distributed computing environment, important data may also be stored on employees' workstations and/or personal computers. Because users may be averse to the hassle of making backups themselves, system administrators must take responsibility for backing up important data stored on employees' computers, in addition to the data stored on central fileservers. Network backup programs such as ADSM from IBM allow system administrators to transparently back up data stored on almost any type of workstation or PC connected to an organization's network. This not only ensures that backups will be performed, but it also causes the backup data to be stored in a uniform way across all computer platforms in use, facilitating easy recovery of lost data.

For small facilities, it makes sense to design a backup system with recovery from both catastrophic failure (e.g., disk failure) and personal error (e.g., a user accidentally deleting an important file) in mind. In terms of absolute number of occurrences, both types of events should be rare at a small site. But for a large facility, the number of personal errors can be huge, swamping the number of large-scale data loss events. For example, in an organization with 10,000 computer users who each lose one file per month, an average of 40 file restorations will be requested each workday. Thus, if a large site wishes to offer "personal error insurance" to its users, administrators should consider augmenting regular backups with a specialized mechanism for recovering accidentally deleted files—preferably one that users can operate themselves. For example, it is possible on many systems to replace the file deletion command with a command that simply moves the "deleted" file into a special per-user directory that is purged periodically (e.g., once each week). A user who accidentally deletes a file can easily restore it by copying it from the special directory into one of the user's regular directories. If this technique is used, system administrators need to get involved (and the backup medium needs to be accessed) only when a user wants to restore a file that was deleted before the last time the special directory was purged. A second example of a user-accessible recovery service is that offered by the AFS distributed filesystem. This filesystem allows users to directly read old versions of their files as regular files stored in a special directory, within certain constraints for how "old" and with some extra disk space consumed compared to that used by a filesystem without this feature. The advantage of this type of user-level file recovery mechanism over the replaced delete command system is that with AFS, users can recover old versions of files they have modified but not deleted.

The frequency with which you should perform regular backups depends on a number of factors. A general guideline is to back up your important data once every 24 hours. Once the backup medium is written to, you must handle it properly. Media should be kept in a locked, fireproof housing (safe, cabinet, etc.), and a second copy of your important data should be maintained offsite. (A number of companies offer offsite data storage for a fee.) System administrators should verify the integrity of backups periodically—horror stories abound of system administrators who thought they were doing a meticulous job of keeping backups only to discover, when a file recovery was finally needed, that all the backup tapes were unusable (e.g., because incorrect parameters were supplied to the backup program). Finally, even if your organization employs only one system administrator, at least a few employees should be familiar with the file backup and restoration process so that backups can continue and files can be restored when the system administrator is on vacation or otherwise not available for an extended period of time. Moreover, a system administrator who knows that other individuals may be performing file restorations is likely to better document the process than one who expects that he or she will be the only one ever to touch the backup tapes.

2.3.1.2 RAID In the case of a catastrophic disk failure that renders an entire disk unreadable, backups can be used to recover the data as it existed at the time of the last backup—but only once the backup tape is located and a spare disk is found. A relatively new technology makes such recovery instantaneous in many cases.

RAID is the concept of using one or more extra disks during the normal operation of a computer system to hold redundant information about the stored files. This redundant information is computed in such a way that should one of the disks in the array fail, all the information stored in the disk array just prior to the failure can be regenerated. Depending on the sophistication of the RAID system employed, it may even be possible to recover from multiple simultaneous disk failures. RAID not only allows essentially instantaneous recovery of lost data, but it also ensures that the recovered data are those on the disk just before the failure—data written since the last backup are not lost.

Although RAID is a very useful technology for environments that demand high availability, RAID does not replace the need for daily backups. First, RAID does not facilitate recovery of a file that has been accidentally or intentionally deleted by an intruder—it only protects against data lost due to disk failure. Second, it does not protect against simultaneous failure of more than a certain number of disks in the array. For example, most RAIDs allow recovery from only one disk failure; if two or more disks fail simultaneously from different causes or, more likely, from the same cause (the cabinet holding the disks falls over during an earthquake, for example), then all the data stored on the disks are lost. Finally, RAID systems are expensive, so they will probably be used to store only an organization's most critical data.

2.3.2 Integrity Data integrity is essential to security. First, it's important that the programs running on your computer systems are actually the programs you think they are, not programs that appear to behave as you expect but that have actually been modified by a malicious individual. (The same applies to system configuration files.) For example, you want to ensure that the login program that authenticates users logging in to the system has not been modified by the addition of a "back door" that allows intruders free access at any time. Second, you want to ensure that the data stored on your system are not modified without your knowledge. For example, if you are performing scientific work and have a file containing thousands of numbers, you might not notice if one value has been changed, though such a change could have serious consequences for your work. Finally, auditing data such as system logs must be maintained unmodified—intruders who can alter the system log can cover their tracks and greatly reduce their chance of being noticed.

There are three solutions to the integrity problem. Each is appropriate in different situations. The first solution, *use of immutable media,* can ensure the integrity of programs and system logs. Two forms of immutable media are CD-ROM and WORM (write once, read many) drives. System programs and configuration files can be kept on either sort of drive (as opposed to a regular disk drive, which can be written to an arbitrary number of times), and system logs can be kept on WORM drives or printed to a printer with a large supply of paper. These approaches use hardware to guarantee that data aren't changed.

Some systems provide *software emulation* of many of the properties of truly immutable media. Depending on the operating system you use and how much you trust it, you may be able to take advantage of so-called *immutable files.* These files can be changed only when a local system administrator reboots the fileserver in a single-user, nonnetworked, administrative mode; this restriction is enforced by the operating system software. Note that this is somewhat less secure than truly immutable media (which are enforced in hardware) because an individual with physical access to the disk can defeat software measures by writing directly to the disk itself; furthermore, you must trust that the operating system will enforce the restrictions on access to immutable files. On the other hand, immutable files require the purchase of no special hardware or software, assuming that the operating system already supports such files. Immutable files can be used to store system programs, configuration files, and data files that you don't want changed. A related sort of file, the *append-only file* (which, as the name suggests, can be appended to but not deleted or otherwise modified), can be used to store system logs. As with immutable files, your operating system may or may not support append-only files.

The third solution to the integrity problem involves cryptography. Cryptography is useful in addressing the integrity of system programs, configuration files, and data files. The idea of this approach is to compute a cryptographically secure *checksum* of each file you wish to protect. A checksum, or *hash*, is a large, fixed length, number that represents the data stored in a file. For integrity protection purposes, the useful properties of cryptographic checksums are: (1) any file is represented by a unique hash, which is computed based on the contents of the file, and (2) if even one bit of the file is changed, the hash will change and in an unpredictable way. If you store on an immutable medium the hashes for the files whose integrity you want to protect, you can always check the integrity of those files by computing their hashes and comparing the values against the values stored on the immutable medium. Any difference indicates the file has been tampered with; a match indicates the file's integrity has been maintained. Because of property (2), it is infeasible for an attacker to replace a valid program with a rogue program that hashes to the same value as did the valid program

Although large enough to be secure, hashes are generally much shorter than the data they represent. Thus, while a hash cannot be used to regenerate the hashed file, the hashes for files can be stored in a fraction of the space needed to store the actual files. For example, using MD5, a popular hashing scheme, the hashes for one thousand files of any size can be stored in less than 16 kilobytes.

The disadvantage of this system over the previous two is that nothing has been done to prevent the files from being tampered with. Cryptography will allow you to detect only that tampering has occurred; it will not restore the file to its original state. However, this is sufficient for many situations, such as operating system software and application programs, which can simply be reinstalled from their original, presumably immutable, media if tampering is detected.

2.3.3 Secrecy The final issue we address related to security of software and data is secrecy, often referred to as confidentiality. Most operating systems support so-called *discretionary access controls*, which allow the owner of a file to specify who can access it. But this does nothing for you if your operating system (or any privileged programs running on it) have security flaws, if an intruder somehow gains privileged access to the system, or if you do not trust your system administrator (who, with most operating systems, can read any file on the system). In light of this, the best way to ensure confidentiality is to use encryption.

2.3.3.1 Discretionary Access Controls Multiuser operating systems generally distinguish among individual users of the system by performing authentication at login time. They subsequently associate an identity with all files created by, or programs run by, a user. Many multiuser operating systems also support the notion of "groups" of users. Associated with each file or device on the system is an owner (generally the user who created the file), a group (generally one of the groups to which the user who created the file belongs), and an indication of who has permission to read, write, and execute (in the case of programs) the file. Discretionary access controls allow users to specify who can access each file they own, and in what way (e.g., read-only; read and write; read and execute; read, write, and execute; etc.).

File access control permissions are an essential part of maintaining confidentiality. Although not as strong a measure as encryption, file permissions are a standard part of commonly used multiuser operating systems and are thus the easiest and most convenient way to ensure privacy of data that are not sensitive.

The most secure default discretionary access control policy is to make all files accessible only by the owner, except for files that must be shared among users. When files must be shared, a group should be established whose membership consists of only those users who need access to the file, and the file should be accessible only to the owner and group. There are few cases in which everyone on a system truly needs access to a file.

Sadly, file access control mechanisms are frequently abused. The easiest way for a user to share files is to simply make them all accessible to "everyone." In this way the user does not have to think about which groups of individuals might need to access which files. Unfortunately, this means that the user is implicitly trusting everyone who has access to, or is able to obtain access to, the system. This includes nosy authorized users as well as unauthorized system intruders. There is no simple solution for this natural tendency to use the easiest way of sharing files—common multiuser operating systems support only "discretionary access control" of the sort previously described, in which the owner of a file decides who can access it. The system administrator can set the permissions on a file, but those permissions can generally be overridden by the file's owner. As a result, user education is the only way to ensure proper use of discretionary access controls.

Mandatory access controls, which solve some of the problems we have mentioned for discretionary access controls, are discussed in section 6.2.1. Mandatory access controls are generally available only in operating systems designed to comply with the most secure rating levels of the government's Trusted Computer Security Evaluation Criteria.

2.3.3.2 Cryptography Encryption is the only way to truly protect sensitive data. Most UNIX systems are shipped with at least two encryption programs, *crypt* and *des*. *crypt* is extremely insecure and should not be used. *des* implements the government's Data Encryption Standard (DES), which is generally regarded as safe if used in the triple-DES mode. (The online documentation about the *des* command will tell you how to invoke the program so that it uses triple-DES.)

Symmetric-key encryption, the type provided by DES, is characterized by the property that the message recipient and sender must share the same secret key in order to communicate. This requires that you set up a shared secret ahead of time with everyone with whom you might wish to communicate securely. This is analogous to laying a telephone wire directly to everyone you'll ever want to call.

Clearly, pure symmetric-key encryption has significant limitations for serious communications security when the number of interconnected computers grows; because of the number of keys involved.But symmetric-key cryptography is ideally suited to file and whole-disk encryption because the person who performs the encryption is likely to be the same person who wants to decrypt it later. One symmetric-key utility of interest is the *encrypting filesystem*, which transparently encrypts files as they are written to disk and decrypts them (given proper user authentication) as they are read from disk. Several implementations of the encrypting filesystem are available for UNIX and PC platforms.

If you encourage your employees to encrypt stored data so as to protect the data from intruders, be aware that recovering a file could be very difficult if the individual who encrypted it leaves the company and refuses to supply the decryption key. Encryption allows disgruntled employees to cause a lot of damage because standard encryption systems do not have a "back door" to allow management to unlock the file if the original encryption key is forgotten or withheld. Special recovery systems, such as commercial key escrow, can solve this problem by ensuring that management always has access to a decryption key. But this sort of system must be set up ahead of time—once an employee has left the company with an encryption key he or she won't disclose, it's too late to implement a key escrow system.

Although symmetric-key encryption is a good way for individuals to protect files and other stored data for their own use, its reliance on a single secret key creates a problem if the file is to be shared among many users. In particular, the secret key would need to be distributed in a secure way to all the individuals needing to share the data. This is the burdensome key management problem, introduced earlier in this section, which cripples symmetric-key encryption when used for large-scale communications security. As a result, protecting *communications* requires a different approach from that used for protecting *stored data*.

PGP (short for Pretty Good Privacy) is one popular cryptosystem for providing communications security. PGP relies on public-key cryptography. In a public-key system, each individual possesses a "private key," which the individual reveals to no one, and its corresponding "public key," which the individual publishes freely. The important properties of public-key cryptography are that (1) data encrypted with an individual's public key can be decrypted only with the corresponding private key and (2) it is considered infeasible to derive the private key of a public-private keypair from the public key of that pair. These properties allow individuals to publish their public keys in a public directory, so that anyone can send messages securely to them but only they can decrypt (and hence read) such messages.

Public-key cryptography enables PGP to scale to a much larger user community than would be possible with symmetric-key encryption because public keys, unlike symmetric keys, can be distributed publicly without compromising security. These characteristics have made public-key cryptography an essential part of almost every large-scale communications security system deployed today. For example, SSL (Secure Sockets Layer), the widespread protocol for secure access to Web servers, relies heavily on public-key cryptography to ensure universal access without predistributed secret keys.

Finally, we offer a warning about buying cryptographic software. Whatever the application, be wary of commercial cryptographic software. It is very difficult for anyone to write flawless cryptographic software, so it pays to check a program's implementation carefully. This is not something that can be done by an unskilled individual or by blind faith in a vendor's untested assertions; you would be wise to utilize the services of a security consultant with a strong knowledge of cryptography when choosing a cryptographic system. It pays to be very careful with all cryptographic software, commercial or freely available. But companies tend to be more secretive about their implementation than do authors of free software, and this makes evaluation of commercial software difficult. If a company claims to use a proprietary encryption algorithm or will not disclose what cryptographic algorithms are used by the program they sell, you would be wise to avoid their products. However, the technical support and user interfaces available in commercial software are typically far superior to anything found in free software; so, as always, a trade-off is involved.

2.3.4 *Audit Logs* Careful logging is essential to the security of your system. Audit logs can be used to detect intruders—be they attackers from outside your company or malicious employees attempting to gain unauthorized access from within—and to determine the extent and type of damage after an attack. Logging can help to deter penetrations if intruders know that they can be traced and caught. Logs, if they are monitored in realtime, can even be used to detect an intrusion in progress. Finally, if you intend to legally prosecute intruders, then audit logs can in some circumstances serve as legal evidence.

Most multiuser operating systems are shipped with a configuration that causes the system to perform some logging of important system events (such as failed login attempts or error messages from system utilities), but additional logging can usually be evoked by making minor changes to one or two system configuration files. Some system utilities are available in a modified form such that they produce logging information beyond what can be obtained using the version of that utility shipped by a system's manufacturer.

The advantage of plentiful log information is clear: the more data available, the greater the chance that a security violation will be indicated by one or more log entries. The disadvantage, though, is that someone or something must read the log entries and separate the important information from the mundane indications that the system is operating properly. A system and/or security administrator should perform this function. In recent years, software that will scan system logs and flag unusual events has become available. (Those conditions considered "unusual" can generally be defined in a configuration file by a system administrator.) This flagging can take the form of electronic mail sent to system operators, paging of system administrators, or even shutting down the system. If such a program is used, the system logs should still be monitored by humans to detect conditions not noticed by the log analysis software.

As discussed in section 2.3.2, audit logs should be stored on an immutable medium. Simply writing log messages to a printer may be sufficient, or more sophisticated techniques such as use of WORM drives may be deemed necessary.

2.3.5 *Viruses, Worms, and Trojan Horses* There are three related computer security dangers that may be unintentionally introduced into your computer systems by unsuspecting users or intentionally introduced by malicious intruders.

2.3.5.1 Viruses During the past decade, the amount of computer software available free or for a nominal charge ("freeware" and "shareware") has skyrocketed. Such programs are frequently distributed through computer networks and bulletin boards. Although these programs have contributed significantly to the productivity and pleasure of computer users around the world, they are subject to computer viruses because of the way they are distributed. The vulnerability of such programs arises from two sources. First, unlike commercial software, whose authors can be easily ascertained, freeware and shareware are almost always subject to unverifiable authorship. A malicious software writer can easily distribute rogue software as freeware or shareware, with little fear of being identified. Second, even software written by well-meaning authors can be tampered with while stored on a bulletin board or Internet file archive site. This tampering can change the nature of the software so that a virus becomes attached to the program.

A *computer virus* is a miniprogram that attaches itself to a larger program, actively infecting other programs and potentially causing other damage whenever the "host" program is invoked. This damage may range from the relatively innocent (e.g., popping up the message "you're infected!" on the user's screen every few months) to the extremely serious (e.g., erasing all the data on the user's computer or, even worse, modifying a few bits of the user's data at a time over a long period, so that the user does not notice the destruction until the situation is uncorrectable). Some viruses trigger immediately the first time the host program runs; others wait until later. Viruses in the latter category are often known as *bombs;* they may initiate their destruction at a particular time (e.g., when the system clock reads Friday the 13th) or upon detecting a particular logical condition in the system (e.g., when the bomb's writer is removed from the company's payroll file). Because of the infectious nature of computer viruses, they can spread rapidly and pose a large threat to your computing infrastructure.

Although traditionally carried by software programs, viruses can also be associated with data files. Since 1995, so-called "macro" viruses have become widespread. Macro viruses affect the users of certain application programs with built-in scripting, or "macro," languages. Examples of such applications include Microsoft Word and Microsoft Excel. A piece of self-replicating code is written in the application's macro language and is attached to, or is made to masquerade as, a regular document for that application. The code is automatically executed when a user performs some operation on the infected document (e.g., opens, closes, or saves it). Besides infecting other documents, the virus can do anything a program written in the application's macro language can do; this generally includes deleting or changing any files the user can access. Virus protection software, discussed later in this section, should be used to protect against macro viruses. Although macro viruses are in some sense just another kind of virus, they require a fundamental change in the way people have traditionally thought about viruses. Viruses can now be spread through files usually considered "data files," such as word processor documents, not just through infected freeware or shareware. As a result, you should scrutinize new documents just as you would new programs.

Computer viruses are primarily a risk to single-user operating systems such as MS-DOS, Microsoft Windows 3.x and 95, and Macintosh OS. A virus that infects such a system has free reign over all files and directories, including the operating system. This freedom allows such viruses to infect other programs and spread easily. By contrast, viruses on multiuser systems that enforce file access controls, such as UNIX, are virtually nonexistent; the strict file access controls tend to contain the spread of would-be viruses and limit the damage they can inflict.

You can help to protect your systems against computer viruses by installing virus protection software. This software will examine an existing system for viruses and, depending on the particular program used, may also examine removable media (e.g., floppy disks) subsequently inserted into the system. Most virus software will not only detect but will also offer to remove viruses found on any disks in or attached to the system.

The downside to virus protection software is that new viruses are constantly written and spread. As a result, virus software must be kept updated with the latest available database of viruses. Such databases are generally available by subscription from the companies that produce virus protection software.

Unfortunately, virus protection software is not infallible. Each year virus writers become more clever at hiding their viruses from antivirus software. There is no 100% guaranteed method to avoid computer viruses, but you can accomplish much by explaining to your users the dangers of viruses and forbidding any circumvention of good virus hygiene.

2.3.5.2 Worms A computer virus "lives" by attaching itself to a piece of "host" software (much as animal viruses live by infecting host cells) but cannot "live" on its own. A *worm*, however, can "survive" by itself. It makes copies of itself and spreads, usually through a computer network. Worms are far less prevalent than viruses, though the most famous computer security incident was in fact a worm attack. The Internet Worm, released in 1988, infected thousands of computers connected to the Internet. The worm was able to spread by exploiting several vulnerabilities in privileged UNIX operating system utilities. Although it significantly degraded the performance of the systems it infected, it did not delete files or do any permanent damage.

It is difficult to generalize about worms because of their scarcity. But ensuring that your operating system has been patched to correct all known security vulnerabilities is an important step in protecting against worms.

2.3.5.3 Trojan Horses The term *Trojan horse* is used to refer to a program that appears innocuous or even beneficial (for example, shareware that the author claims will optimize your hard drive performance) but is in fact destructive. The program may even appear to behave as advertised while silently violating system security in some way (it may cause direct damage, such as deleting files, or indirect damage, such as sending an electronic mail message to someone outside your company listing all the software installed on the computer it has attacked). A Trojan horse may hide a virus that is released into the system when the Trojan horse program is first invoked.

The best protection against Trojan horses is much the same as the best protection against computer viruses—ensure that software you install is initially free of malicious potential, and then protect it from modification using the techniques described in section 2.3.2.

2.3.5.4 General Protective Techniques Because viruses and trojan horses are generally introduced unknowingly by an organization's employees when they bring software into the company from an external source, they are very difficult to protect against. Viruses have even infected commercial software by attacking one or more computers used by software developers at a vendor's company, and then later spreading when the developed software is duplicated for distribution and sale. You can minimize your risk, however, by installing only commercial software on machines running single-user operating systems and by carefully checking into the security history of freeware or shareware installed on multiuser systems.

If you must install freeware or shareware on a machine running a single-user operating system, check the software with a virus scanner first. Install virus-checking software on all such systems. On multiuser systems, system administrators should be careful never to run untrusted software from a privileged system account. Finally, cryptographic checksums are increasingly being distributed with commercial, freeware, and shareware software; if the checksum you receive from the author is digitally signed by the author and matches the checksum of the software installed, you at least know that the program was not modified between the time it was examined by the author and the time you received it. Although this doesn't prevent a virus or trojan horse, it does help you narrow down the field of individuals who might be to blame if you later find that the program caused a security violation.

2.3.6 Security and the World Wide Web During the past few years the popularity of the World Wide Web has exploded. Indeed, the Web has quickly become the driving force behind the Internet's rapid growth. Companies around the world have made information about their products and services available to the public through their Web sites. Researchers frequently make their publications available online via the Web. Many traditional media services such as newspapers, magazines, and television and radio broadcasters have set up Web sites that provide information similar to that available in the more traditional media formats. And as Web technology advances, Web sites are increasingly offering users the option not only to read about a company's products and services, but also to purchase those products and services directly via the Web.

There are many reasons why your employees might want to use the Web in the course of their daily work. If nothing else, the Web is a great way for them to stay informed about what your competitors are doing (or at least what your competitors are doing and are willing to publicize!).

Unfortunately, there are some dangers associated with Web "browsing." These dangers have to do with "active content"—miniprograms that are embedded within some Web pages. When a Web page with active content is viewed, the embedded program is executed on the viewer's computer. Several languages are commonly used today to provide active content on Web pages. The best known are Java, JavaScript, and ActiveX. The detailed security issues related to these languages are complex and outside the scope of this booklet. We refer the interested reader to *Java Security: Hostile Applets, Holes, and Antidotes* by Gary McGraw and Edward W. Felten (New York: John Wiley and Sons, 1997).

Put simply, there are security risks associated with all three of these active content languages. These risks do not necessarily exceed those of simply downloading a program from the Internet and executing it on your computer. But the danger of active content lies in the fact that it is much easier to fool an unsuspecting user into downloading and executing a Java program, a JavaScript script, or an ActiveX control than it is to fool the same user into downloading a program using a standard file transfer protocol and then executing that program by hand. With the click of a button, unsuspecting Web users can download and begin to run a program that compromises the security of their own machines and possibly those of other systems on their company's internal network, without even realizing what they have done. Like macro viruses (see section 2.3.5.1), active Web content blurs the distinction between what is a "program" and what is a "document." For maximum safety, assume that any piece of information that enters your computer has the potential to cause damage, and plan your defenses accordingly.

The two most popular Web browsers available today (a "browser" is the program used to read Web pages and to navigate through Web sites), Netscape Navigator and Microsoft Internet Explorer, allow users to disable execution of active content by the browser. We recommend that you disable active content execution within your Web browser if you want maximum protection from the threat of malicious active content.

2.4 Protecting Networks

These days, many computers used in businesses and other organizations are connected to networks, and more become connected every day. The standalone workstation is quickly becoming a relic of the past.

Computer networks can be LANs, which connect computers within a single organization, or "wide-area networks" (WANs), which connect local-area networks. In this section, we concentrate on WANs, in particular, the Internet, because network security concerns are much more serious when a network is accessible to the entire world than when it is accessible only to users within a particular company.

Even if your company is not connected to the Internet, you may still have concerns about network security within your organization. For example, you may wish to protect the computers on the portion of your LAN within the payroll division from computers on other portions of the corporate LAN. In such cases, the information in this section, though geared toward protecting against attacks from the Internet, can be interpreted as techniques for protecting a sensitive part of your corporate LAN from untrusted portions.

If your corporate LAN is connected to the Internet or you're considering an Internet connection, then the information in this section is vital. Many computer users and businesses now depend on access to the tremendous resources available on the Internet. Unfortunately, the same vastness and openness that make the Internet such a useful tool also result in its serving as home to many potential intruders and troublemakers. In this section, we identify several techniques for protecting your organization's internal network from external attack.

2.4.1 *Controlling Connectivity* The simplest way to stop network intrusions is to carefully control the level of connectivity between your internal computer resources and machines in the outside world. After all, if intruders cannot reach your machines via some network path, they will find it impossible to mount a network-based attack on you.

We presume that you already have, or plan to have, computers for internal use. We expect that you have, or plan to have, an internal network for those machines. Finally, we expect that you are considering obtaining some level of Internet connectivity or modifying your current level of Internet connectivity. This presents a conundrum replete with trade-offs between security and flexibility. We describe four basic approaches to limiting connectivity and then elaborate on a few possible enhancements.

2.4.1.1 Connectivity Approach 1: Unrestricted Connectivity If you weren't worried about security, you might simply connect your internal network directly to the Internet, with no restrictions on connectivity. Unfortunately, this approach provides very poor protection because it forces each machine on your network to protect itself from network attacks—there is no central or group defense against such attacks. Moreover, the default out-of-the-box configuration provided for computer systems from most vendors often provides weak security at best. As a result, unless a system administrator has spent a good deal of time tweaking the default system software and installing special software to protect each machine on your network, your networked workstations will provide very little resistance to a network intrusion. Furthermore, even if software has been installed to make a networked system "secure," the task of routine administration of your machines' security software is a heavy burden that must be borne by the system administrator of each machine separately. In short, there are large practical difficulties involved in setting up and maintaining a collection of secure machines on a large scale. In practice, many of your machines will be vulnerable to network attack if you opt for unrestricted Internet connectivity.

The minimal security afforded by unrestricted connectivity might be appropriate in some low-security environments, such as small organizations with little online information of value or universities dedicated to maintaining an open computing environment suitable for research. Many universities use special software on each host they wish to protect. This software allows system administrators to specify which machines on the Internet may connect to those protected hosts and which system services may be accessed remotely. But because of the time that must be spent maintaining this software on each protected machine, the reliance that must be placed on the software's proper operation, and the need to specify individually which services on which machines are to be protected, we classify this approach as "unrestricted connectivity." Unrestricted connectivity is a very dangerous configuration; those who use it should expect network intrusions. We discourage organizations that regularly rely on their computers and online data from employing this approach—the risks are unbounded.

2.4.1.2 Connectivity Approach 2: No Connectivity One possible reaction to the dangers of full connectivity is to permit no Internet connectivity. Strict disconnection provides strong assurance that your internal machines will be safe from external network attacks. It also means, however, that you lose access to all the resources available on the Internet. For some very high security organizations, this may be appropriate, but most organizations do not fall into this category. Given the ever-increasing popularity and pervasiveness of the Internet, complete disconnection is an extreme and, for almost all conceivable organizations, highly undesirable solution.

In any case, complete disconnection can be difficult to implement. Employees who are dissatisfied with this policy might decide to attach modems to their office workstations and use them to connect to the Internet. If their workstations are willing to act as routers—as many are—your internal network is suddenly connected to the entire Internet. In this way, one employee can single-handedly subvert your network connectivity policy.

There are many frightening stories of this effect circulating within the security community. For instance, Brent Chapman, an expert on network firewalls, related the following story (with additional details provided by Dan Geer). One employee of a large organization worked from home, and his wife telecommuted to another large organization. The pair had built a small LAN consisting of their two home computers; soon the ISDN lines that connected each of their computers to their employers' internal networks became saturated with all the traffic flowing between the internal networks of the two organizations—even though the organizations' security policies required such traffic to pass through the organizations' respective firewalls. (Firewalls are discussed in section 2.4.1.4.) The routers had silently discovered that routing through the home LAN was more efficient than traversing the two firewalls. Unbeknownst to security officers at either corporation, those two well-meaning, knowledgeable engineers had unwittingly compromised their companies' security policies.

The fundamental problem with disconnection is that it is fragile. Internet routing protocols are designed to robustly route around disconnections, and even a single, low-bandwidth link to the outside world can entirely negate all your efforts to keep your internal network isolated from outsiders. Because complete disconnection is such an extreme solution, universal employee cooperation with such a restrictive policy is likely to be very difficult to achieve.

2.4.1.3 Connectivity Approach 3: Dual Networks One possible response to risk is to transfer the risk to someone else and to let him or her manage it. In the context of network security, one can effect a risk transfer by using someone else's system for all Internet communications. The easiest way to do this is to buy accounts on the system of an Internet Service Provider (ISP) for all your employees. Your internal network should be disconnected from the Internet (for example, your internal machines should be made strictly inaccessible from the ISP). In this way, you can safely use your internal LAN or network for intraorganizational work while providing Internet access for your workers. If the ISP is compromised, your internal network and the data on it remain secure by virtue of its disconnection. (Of course, you should warn employees not to store valuable proprietary information on the insecure ISP accounts, unless you trust the ISP's site security very highly.) While this solution allows employees to access the Internet, it rules out any direct connection between the organization's internal network and the Internet and hence provides a high level of safety.

A related approach maintains the strict separation of your internal LAN from external networks. But instead of using an ISP to provide Internet access, your organization uses its own equipment to provide Internet access for its employees while keeping that equipment completely isolated from the company's internal LAN. The advantage of this approach over the previous one is that your organization may be able to offer Internet access to employees more cost effectively by essentially becoming an ISP for the employees than by purchasing accounts through a third-party ISP. You should also consider whether it would be easier to maintain strict separation between the ISP's network and the internal corporate network if the networks are hosted by different organizations or by a single organization.

The approaches based on strict segregation of dual networks have some limitations. If your employees' workloads can be divided into portions that require intraorganization communication and those that involve interaction with outside parties via the Internet, this approach will work well. But many organizations do not fit this model. Imagine giving your employees two telephones, one for calling inside the company and one for dialing outside. Would this be practical in your organization? The strict segregation of dual networks works well in preventing an outsider from compromising proprietary stored data, but it also limits online communication. Finally, we note the difficulty of completely disconnecting your internal network, as discussed in section 2.4.1.2.

The previous few paragraphs assume that you want to provide actual Internet access to your employees. Some organizations might not need direct employee Internet access and might instead be satisfied with simply establishing an Internet presence via, for example, a Web server. This gives your organization visibility on the Internet (and all the advertising and public relations benefits such visibility entails) without the risks of connecting the organization's LAN directly to the Internet. The two approaches discussed earlier in this section can be adapted to this situation—you can isolate your internal network from the Web server so that compromise of the Web server does not threaten your internal network. Much as before, the host on which the Web server runs could be either operated by an external ISP or located on a machine that your organization operates and maintains.

2.4.1.4 Connectivity Approach 4: Limited Access If unrestricted connectivity is too dangerous for your organization, but no connectivity and separate networks are too limiting, then you'll probably be interested in a fourth approach, limited access. This policy, arguably the most commonly used by commercial organizations today, allows partial connectivity between your internal network and the Internet by screening connections between computers within your organization and those outside. The device that performs this screening is known as a *firewall.* It serves as a central, closely guarded gateway through which all Internet connections must pass; the only way data can move from your organization to the outside world, or vice versa, is through the firewall.

Firewalls have become one of the hottest topics in Internet security. Entire books have been written about firewalls, and we cannot attempt to do the subject full justice in this booklet. Instead, we offer a brief introduction to firewalls—enough to help you decide whether a firewall is appropriate for your situation—and refer you to other references for more information. Two excellent books on the subject are *Firewalls and Internet Security: Repelling the Wily Hacker* by William R. Cheswick and Steven Bellovin (Reading, MA: Addison-Wesley Longman, 1994), a thorough treatment of the philosophy, theory, and implementation of firewalls from two highly respected security gurus, and *Building Internet Firewalls* by D. Brent Chapman and Elizabeth D. Zwicky (Sebastopol, CA: O'Reilly & Associates, 1995), a down-to-earth cookbook for implementing firewalls with a very comprehensive list of the nitty-gritty technical details you'll need to confront when building a firewall.

A firewall is a tool for enforcing a *security perimeter.* Consider an analogy to physical security: to protect the contents of a building, one might establish a security checkpoint at each entrance to the building but install very few defenses within the building. Network security with firewalls is based on the same idea: one delimits a security perimeter and carefully guards all attempts to cross it without worrying too much about protecting network traffic that stays entirely within the perimeter.

The fundamental motivation for a firewall is simple: many organizations need flexible and secure Internet access, but the burden of securing every internal computer is simply too great for any but the smallest organization. By using a firewall, an organization can establish a central choke point to carefully guard the internal machines. In this way, the organization can concentrate its resources on securing the firewall machine, instead of having to spread those resources among all computers on the internal network.

An example of how a firewall works will help to explain its function. A firewall might allow email communications to pass freely between the internal network and the Internet. It might also allow internal users to browse external Web sites unrestricted. A typical firewall will prevent an outsider from initiating a login connection to an internal machine. A more sophisticated firewall might allow a login connection to an internal machine to be initiated from an external machine only if the connection has been authenticated with an organization-issued hardware token; one of the values of firewalls is to help centralize enforcement of policy decisions such as this one. (For more information on secure user authentication techniques, see section 2.2.) The firewall can also ensure that outsiders can't access your internal fileservers and Web servers.

A firewall is a cost-effective tool for implementing certain types of security policies. Unfortunately, there seems to exist a widespread attitude in some poorly informed organizations that "you need a firewall to be secure, and once you have one, you needn't worry about security anymore." This is a serious misunderstanding of the value of firewalls, and we strongly urge you to avoid this trap. Your firewall may be the centerpiece of your organization's security implementation, but it should by no means be the only protective measure you take. Firewalls can fail, and the software they run can have security bugs. You should therefore protect internal machines enough to limit the damage intruders can do if they manage to get past your firewall. Also realize that not all firewalls are created equal: the word "firewall" spans a great spectrum of security gateways, from inexpensive routers that provide only the simplest protection to highly sophisticated, super-secure filtering gateways. If you decide that a firewall is appropriate, make sure you pick one that matches your security policy. Finally, always remember that a firewall is merely a tool for implementing policy, not a substitute for a good security policy.

2.4.1.5 A Final Note on Controlling Connectivity Restricting Internet access to and from your organization via any of the means we have described is bound to improve your organization's security. But it's important to remember that these techniques are designed to prevent malicious outsiders from finding and exploiting security vulnerabilities in the computer systems connected to your organization's LAN. They can't prevent a malicious employee from leaking secret corporate information outside the organization. Firewalls are generally configured to allow internal users to make connections outside the organization, through which they could send proprietary information. Use of dual networks makes the job only slightly more difficult—employees can copy data from their workstations connected to the internal network onto floppy disks, put those floppy disks into their computers connected to external networks, and send the data wherever they please. Finally, even in the case of no Internet connectivity, employees can copy data from their workstations onto floppy disks and carry the disks out the door on their way out of the building at the end of the day. Our point: technical solutions to security problems can go a long way toward preventing attack from outside, but there is very little one can do to prevent employees from maliciously transferring information out of the organization, except preventing employees from gaining access to the information in the first place. (How to do the latter via technical means is discussed in section 2.3.3.)

2.4.2 *Cryptographic Protection of Network Traffic* Limiting Internet connectivity is a useful technique to stop attackers from exploiting vulnerabilities of the computer systems connected to your organization's LAN. But that's not the whole story of network security. There is another class of threats that must be dealt with differently. When data travel on an open network such as the Internet, adversaries can snoop on and/or tamper with legitimate connections; the example of "connection hijacking" was described in section 2.2.3. For example, when an internal user connects to an outside Web server, malicious hackers on the Internet could eavesdrop on the Web data or send back a bogus Web page. As another example, email transmitted over the Internet is not secure: outsiders can easily eavesdrop on or even forge their own messages. Threats such as eavesdropping and message tampering cannot be addressed by firewalls.

Several countermeasures are available. One approach is to simply warn your users not to trust anything received from (or sent to) the Internet; of course, this education process is easier said than done. Unfortunately, this approach is not applicable to all environments: if your organization wants to use the Internet to connect its offices in multiple cities, wants to exchange business information with another organization through the Internet, or wants to take orders from customers via email or the World Wide Web, you will need to depend on data that travel over the open Internet. Under such circumstances, some method of verifying the integrity of data received from an external network is needed. Judicious application of cryptography is precisely the right solution.

Encryption of data transmitted over the Internet protects the confidentiality of communications and prevents passive eavesdropping. Cryptographic authentication of an entire connection (including all data packets, not just the initial connection request) stops message tampering and connection hijacking. When both integrity *and* confidentiality of your communications are required, encryption and authentication can be combined. We treat encryption and authentication together in the following paragraphs only as they relate to protecting network data. Section 2.3.3.2 discusses the use of cryptography to protect data stored on disk.

Cryptography is a powerful technique for preserving the confidentiality of sensitive communications. But it has only recently started to see widespread deployment in common Internet systems.

One of the first practical systems to implement automatic message encryption was MIT's Kerberos system. Kerberos is designed to address the difficult security problem of insider attack. Kerberos replaces standard network utilities with program versions that incorporate strong user authentication as well as full (but optional) connection encryption. Kerberos does not attempt to address issues like end-to-end email security; it encrypts and authenticates data packets passing between machines rather than whole messages. The main disadvantages of Kerberos are twofold: it is not well suited for interorganization traffic, and it requires work by system administrators to modify the software installed on every computer in the organization. Kerberos itself is more of a tool than a product, but it is the basis of DCE, the Distributed Computing Environment from the Open Software Foundation, which is a full-fledged product. To its credit, Kerberos incorporates the only fully implemented key distribution system for symmetric cryptography, and it is used by the most demanding sites.

More recently, many application-specific encryption technologies have been developed for login sessions, Web traffic, and electronic mail. SSH ("Secure SHell"), which encrypts login sessions, does not come standard with any current systems, but is freely available on the Internet. SSL, which provides encryption and authentication for Web traffic, is supported by most popular Web browsers such as those from Netscape and Microsoft. An increasing number of Web servers are taking advantage of SSL to protect communication with browsers. Finally, PGP, which offers encryption and authentication for electronic mail, is built into an increasing number of electronic mail software packages. A small amount of installation work is required whether PGP is built into a mail program or used by itself, but this installation can be done without system administrator intervention.

Systems such as Kerberos, SSL, and PGP all fall into the category of "application-layer" cryptography because encryption, decryption, and authentication are performed by an application program. By contrast, IPv6, introduced in section 2.2.1, will incorporate encryption and authentication at the network level. Because it will be built into the operating system instead of individual applications, this security mechanism will be able to encrypt and authenticate all Internet packets. It will thus protect any application that uses the network, without requiring modification to individual applications. Application-level security will remain important, however, because it can offer features specific to an application, going beyond the generic security offered by a network protocol.

2.4.3 A Special Warning for ISPs

As public interest in the Internet has grown, the number of companies providing Internet access has exploded. Unfortunately, the individuals who operate Internet Service Provider companies are not always aware of the severe security threats facing the equipment they use to provide that access. The biggest security problem for ISPs is that by design they give the general public (their customers) computer system and LAN access. Worse, they often do this without any verification or screening of customers' identities. Because gaining user-level access is usually the first step in compromising a system, providing such access to the general public means inviting a potential intentional human threat and even helping one get started. There is no need for a social engineering attack when all a potential intruder has to do is promise to pay for an account. An ISP is in the business of providing Internet connectivity, so such connectivity is usually unrestricted by definition. Thus, from an ISP customer account, a malicious user can often launch "insider" attacks on the ISP or use the ISP systems to launch attacks on other organizations, for example by sniffing the passwords of other ISP customers. Both possibilities present a substantial threat to the business of the ISP, and both have occurred in practice. As a result, ISPs must take special care to:

- restrict systems on which customer access is provided and consider eliminating system command-line ("shell") access altogether

- protect customers' data from other customers and from other individuals on the Internet

- protect noncustomer internal production systems and data from both customers and the Internet

- validate the identities of customers *prior* to granting access, to enhance accountability and to aid incident response

2.5 User Education and the Risks of Social Engineering

Computer security, like a chain, is only as strong as its weakest link. In many organizations, system users are the weakest link in the security chain. No matter how many technical defenses your organization deploys, users may intentionally or unintentionally act in ways that compromise security. *Social engineering* is a technique used to exploit the one nontechnical information security vulnerability every organization possesses: its employees.

In a social engineering attack, an adversary takes advantage of the fact that most employees are not very aware of security issues and as a result are often willing to reveal security-critical information about the organization. For example, some employees might disclose their password to anyone who calls them on the telephone claiming to be from the company's computer security department. Or a malicious hacker might bypass your sophisticated firewall by phoning your company's Help Desk, posing as a new employee and asking for the phone number of the modem pool so as to dial in to work from home.

Unfortunately, much personal information about an organization's employees can often be deduced from its Web server(s), online phone books, and other publicly available data. These sources may yield enough information to allow an attacker to convince an employee that the attacker is also an employee of the organization. Other favorite attack techniques include gaining physical access to a company's computer resources by posing as a repair technician or by obtaining a job as a janitor. Those who attack using social engineering are con artists, and when they're trying to make their way into your organization's computer resources, the stakes are very high.

Social engineering is a significant threat, and it is not new. Horror stories abound. Phone "phreakers" (individuals who obtain information about telephone systems and sometimes use that information for fraudulent purposes) have successfully used social engineering techniques to walk off with proprietary technical manuals detailing the inner workings of the telephone system. Not long after the Clinton administration announced that Mykotronx Inc. had been awarded a contract to build the controversial Clipper Chip, an anonymous party sifted through Mykotronx's garbage (an activity known as "dumpster diving") and retrieved and published several key internal documents containing information such as salaries, itemized year-to-date company expenses, and employee lists. Incidents of forged "security advisories" forced CERT to start signing their advisories using PGP authentication. An academic paper, "Information Security Technology? Don't Rely on It. A Case Study in Social Engineering," by Ira S. Winkler and Brian Dealy (5th USENIX UNIX Security Symposium, 1995), reports the result of an internal security test conducted by the authors. Using social engineering techniques, they obtained access to internal employee phone books, modem pool phone numbers, account names, passwords, and other information in just three days of telephone calling. Is your organization equally vulnerable?

Even more insidious than social engineering attacks from outside your organization is the possibility that internal users may inadvertently cause security problems simply because they don't know better. For instance, if your organization has a very restrictive firewall or dial-in modem policy, employees may connect modems to their workstations at work so that they can dial in from a computer at home to do work, thus unintentionally creating the possibility of serious security loopholes. As another example, malicious hackers once announced a "convenient" service: they told employees of a company that they would install a useful program for the employees if the employees would just type a command that, although the victims did not realize it, would let the hackers issue arbitrary commands in the victim's account, as long as the organization's firewall allowed connections to be made from internal company computers to computers on the Internet (as most firewalls do). Even well-meaning employees, if they are not properly educated about security threats and policies, can cause serious security problems without realizing it.

An ounce of prevention is worth a pound of cure, and the best general way to mitigate the risks of social engineering, dumpster diving, users inadvertently creating vulnerabilities, and the like is education. Users need to be taught about basic attitudes and issues related to information security. Employees need to know the importance of keeping their password secret, even if corporate officers send email or call on the telephone by asking for it. Users need to know basic facts about email and Web security. Instilling the right attitude and a healthy dose of prudent paranoia is the best way to prevent employees from accidentally compromising security. A program of security awareness training is vital to a serious computer security implementation.

There are several additional countermeasures you can deploy to help defend specifically against social engineering. The paper by Winkler and Dealy on social engineering offers several recommendations:

- Educate your users: teach basic security practices.

- Don't rely on employee ID numbers (or other commonly used internal identifiers) for employee authentication over the phone, computer, etc.

- Before disclosing confidential or proprietary information to supposed employees, check the phone number they are calling from: look them up in the employee telephone directory and call them back, or use CallerID. Analogous procedures can help prevent email spoofing.

- Appoint computer support analysts: all users should be personally familiar with their designated analyst and should immediately contact the analyst if anyone else approaches them via electronic mail, the telephone, etc., claiming to be from the organization's computer support department.

- Create an organization-wide security alert system so that all users can be warned if an attempted social engineering attack is in progress.

- Assess site security: have trusted security professionals attempt to gain access using social engineering techniques in carefully monitored tests.

In addition to employee education, it also helps to remember the legitimate needs of your users when designing and implementing a security policy. Don't make security measures so stifling that users look for ways to get around them in order to get work done. Engineers can be very creative at solving problems, and if your security controls are viewed as a problem, then that problem is likely to get solved—much to your dismay. In short, make sure that your security policy is widely accepted, avoid overly restrictive security measures, and institute computer security education and awareness programs.

3.0 Financial Considerations and Risk Management

This section is a brief introduction to *risk analysis*. Risk analysis is a tool to help you understand the financial ramifications of security threats and to evaluate what level of security controls are needed in your organization. We will use the following terms in discussing risk analysis:

access compromise—the gaining of unauthorized access to a physical location or piece of information

annual frequency estimate (AFE)—the estimated number of times a particular threat will occur in a single year

asset—anything that has monetary or intellectual value

data integrity—keeping data safe from modification or destruction

data confidentiality—keeping data secret from people/programs not authorized to have access to it

threat—"Any force or phenomenon that could degrade the availability, integrity, or confidentiality of an Automated Data Processing (ADP) resource, system or network" (Federal Information Processing Standard FIPS PUB 65, "Guidelines for Automatic Data Processing Analysis," U.S. Department of Commerce National Institute of Standards and Technology, 1979).

risk—used interchangeably with threat; see previous definition

security control/safeguard—a control or safety mechanism, be it physical (e.g., a door lock), procedural (e.g., a policy), or technical (e.g., a computer program) that prevents a potential threat or limits its impact

vulnerability—a weakness or error in a system or program that can be exploited to gain access to the system or data

Determining exactly how much and what type of security your organization needs is not an easy task, nor is it one that should be taken lightly. Before you can know what security controls to implement, you must determine what assets your organization wishes to protect, how much they are worth, and what threats to them exist. This information, combined with your organization's computer security philosophy (for example, what degree of security precautions your employees will tolerate), will help you determine what security controls should be enacted. This process is commonly referred to as a *risk analysis*. The goal of a risk analysis is to strike an appropriate balance between the threats that exist and the security controls that can help minimize them. A natural side effect of this process will be determining which risks are acceptable and which should be limited or prevented.

Find the right balance between protection and employee productivity and between the cost of protection and the value of the protected assets is a challenge. A state of total security, one in which all risks have been eliminated, will never exist. Computer security is about finding the right level of caution necessary to meet the needs of the organization and understanding the consequences of the risks the organization has chosen to accept. In the end, decisions regarding security are made by weighing the dollars spent to achieve the desired level of security (in terms of purchasing security equipment and software, paying employees to install and operate such equipment, and lost productivity of employees who are occasionally hampered in their normal work by security measures) against the risk reduction achieved.

The risk analysis process is divided into five steps:

1. Identify assets and their associated cost.

2. Identify threats and their frequency.

3. Identify security controls in place.

4. Identify the weaknesses and areas of concern.

5. Make recommendations for a course of action.

Ten years ago, formal risk analysis was the norm, especially in government-related organizations. A formal risk analysis would include evaluating all assets and all possible threats to those assets. For large organizations, such a process might take many months and might not be cost-effective. People faced with this enormous task often chose to outsource the job to a consulting company, sometimes paying $10,000 to $20,000 for the complete project and report. Today, formal risk analyses are inappropriate for many organizations. Technology advances too rapidly for such reports to remain relevant for long once they are issued, and many companies are in a continual growth process. An informal risk analysis performed by the organization itself, which considers only major assets and the most likely threats, is often the preferred analysis method.

If you decide to take on the risk analysis task yourself with the help of your technical staff, you may wish to use a software package that helps to automate the process. The following are three such packages:

ARES (Automated Risk Evaluation System)

BDSS (Bayesian Decision Support System)

CRAMM (CCTA Risk Analysis and Management Methodology)

As a manager, your first task is to determine the level of risk analysis you wish to perform and whether you want the work done in-house or by an outside consulting company. The goals and size of your organization will play a part in your decision. If a previous risk analysis has been done at your organization, your task will be much easier; but if you are doing one for the first time, be prepared for a lot of work.

This section is not meant as an in-depth description of how to perform a risk analysis. Rather, our goal is to provide enough of an overview to help you determine the size of the task and to present you with some ideas that might apply to your organization. For a more in-depth discussion of formal risk analysis, we offer the following resources: Baker, R. H. *Network Security: How to Plan and Achieve It.* (Berkeley, CA: McGraw-Hill, 1995); Fites, M., Katz, P., and Brebner, A. *Control and Security of Computer Information Systems.* (Potomac, MD: Computer Science Press, 1989); Pfleeger, C. *Security in Computing*, 2nd ed. (Upper Saddle River, NJ: Prentice-Hall, 1996); and Stang, D. *Network Security Secrets.* (Foster City, CA: IDG Books, 1993).

3.1 Identifying Your Assets

The first step of a risk analysis is to identify the assets you want to protect and to determine their value. In an informal risk analysis, one typically identifies only the major assets and estimates the value of the remaining, smaller assets lumped into a single category (such as all removable CD-ROM drives). Many organizations have strict property tracking and identification procedures; some even have property management databases that list all tagged property, including the make, model, cost, and depreciation value. If your organization has a property management database, the task of identifying assets will be much easier.

Assets should be divided into several categories; for example:

physical assets

    computers

    network equipment

    storage media

    building structures

intellectual assets

    program code and documentation

    input data

    information on World Wide Web pages

database information

design plans

intangible assets

company reputation

employee morale

privacy of users

information confidentiality

computer services and processes

disk drive resources

CPU allocation

support staff

The easy part of identifying and valuing assets is to specify the organization's physical assets and to place a cost on them. (The cost should reflect the replacement price should you need to purchase that item again today.) The difficult part is determining what significant intellectual property your organization possesses and which intangible assets are key resources. Intellectual property and intangible assets often play a major role in the success of your organization, so you should plan to protect against their loss.

3.2 Identifying the Threats

The next stage of the risk analysis involves identifying the threats to your assets. Threats are generally classified into four areas:

1. intentional human threats (e.g., vandalism)

2. accidental human threats (e.g., janitor spills coffee on your computer)

3. natural environmental threats (e.g., earthquake, flood)

4. fabricated environmental threats (e.g., power spike destroys your fileserver)

Some of these threats were discussed in sections 2.1–2.3. If you are new to the risk analysis process, you might be unaware of the more uncommon or obscure threats. Some resources that can help you with this process are: Holbrook, P. and Reynolds, J. "Site Security Handbook." Internet RFC 1244. Internet Engineering Task Force, 1991; Braud, R. "Coping with the Threat of Computer Security Incidents: A Primer for Prevention through Recovery." *ftp://ftp.cert.org/pub/primer.txtr*, and "UNIX Security Frequently Asked Questions," maintained by Christopher Klaus at *ftp://iss.net.*

Some security and risk analysis experts feel that every site faces the same set of threats, just with different levels of frequency. Whatever the threats may be, you should ask yourself the following questions:

What is threatened (integrity, confidentiality, accessibility, reputation, safety)?

Is the threat preventable and is the cost of prevention worth the benefit?

How can you detect that the threat has been exploited?

What is the severity of the threat (how much damage will be done and how much will it cost to recover from it)?

3.2.1 *Intentional Human Threats* One of the more obvious types of threats is intentional human threats. These are deliberate acts against a computer resource for such reasons as personal gain, revenge, sabotage, fun, or the challenge of defeating "the system." Some of the more common intentional human threats are:

- impersonation (e.g., a person using someone else's account)
- password guessing
- network attack that takes advantage of vulnerabilities in network protocols
- remote network access compromise
- misuse of computer resources by users/employees (e.g., playing games)
- unauthorized browsing (e.g., an employee viewing a manager's electronic mailbox)
- exploiting operating system vulnerabilities
- trojan horses, worms, and viruses (discussed in section 2.3.5)
- system impersonation (someone installs a rogue computer on your network and causes it to masquerade as a valid host)
- theft of assets

These threats will probably constitute the majority of your security concerns because computer security is mainly a "people problem"—most security violations are perpetrated by insiders.

Procedural and technical controls that can help prevent or reduce these threats are discussed in sections 2.1–2.3.

One should also consider less common intentional human threats such as:

fraud and embezzlement

vandalism

arson

strike or labor dispute

3.2.2 *Accidental Human Threats* Accidental human threats form the second class of "people problems." These are unintentional acts that cause damage to computing resources by introducing erroneous data, omitting required data, or violating proper procedures. Most often these threats are due to improper training, carelessness, or ignorance. Some examples of accidental human threats are:

- operation errors that result from failure to follow (or understand) procedures (e.g., booting a system improperly, inserting the wrong backup tape, or issuing an incorrect command that destroys data)
- system programming errors
- data destruction or disclosure due to improper permissions on files or accidental removal of a file
- accidental physical damage to computer equipment (spilling liquids on electronic parts, accidentally unplugging the power cord from a computer that is turned on and operating, dropping a piece of equipment, etc.)

Many accidental human threats can be prevented through good training, proper procedures, and quality assurance programs. Accidents are bound to happen occasionally, but their frequency and impact can be reduced.

3.2.3 *Environmental Threats* Environmental threats can be either natural or fabricated. Natural environmental threats will often vary according to geographical region. Some examples of natural environmental threats are:

floods

severe storms or high winds

major earthquakes

tornadoes

electrical storms

hurricanes

Fabricated environmental threats are those events caused by failure of a component in the computing environment. Such threats include:

air conditioning failure

water leakage

power failure

hardware failure

network or communication failure

Although environmental threats cannot always be avoided, preventative measures can be taken to minimize damage and loss. Some methods to combat environmental threats are discussed in section 2.1.1.

3.3 Threat Frequency and Impact

Estimating the frequency of the threats you have identified is the next phase of the risk analysis. Unfortunately, this can be the most difficult aspect of the entire process. Establishing a frequency and cost value for some threats can mean playing a guessing game. If they are available, use statistics from your own organization or comparable facilities; if you are not currently keeping records and logs of such events, then start doing so. In some cases, agencies such as local law enforcement or incident response organizations like CERT or CIAC (see appendix B for contact information) may be able to provide you with statistics on frequency of occurrence and dollar loss resulting from specific incidents. Insurance and audit companies may also be able to provide such information.

When estimating the frequency of threats, you need to determine how many times the threat is likely to occur in a single year (often referred to as the AFE). Some events, e.g., major earthquake, may happen only once every 50 years in certain geographical regions. Some threats may occur as much as once per day or more. For example, "door knocks," tests conducted by outsiders via the Internet to find out what security measures an organization has in place, happen daily (or even many times a day) at some sites. At the end of the frequency estimate phase, you will have an AFE associated with each threat on your list.

Next you must determine the impact of each threat. Again, this may be somewhat difficult. Damage to physical property as the result of a fire or water leakage is easy to associate with a cost. But if someone installs a network sniffer on your network and captures 20,000 username/password pairs, the level of damage is not as obvious. In these cases, you need to look at what is done with the information and what will be needed to restore your environment to an acceptable level of security. Sometimes just a "visitation" by an intruder who enters illegally and looks around, but does not modify anything can lead to many hours of work by a system administrator to audit the systems involved and to review the appropriate system logs just to ensure that no damage was done. Even if no "real" damage was done, there will be a cost associated with the incident, not to mention a loss of confidence in your organization's security.

Another gray area in determining loss involves intellectual property and intangible items. If someone walks out with an 8 mm tape containing all of your company's source code and design plans and gives this information to a competing company, what is the loss? Perhaps the eventual product would have been a complete failure, in which case the loss is not so great. But the product could have been a substantial success, in which case the loss could be huge. What if an intruder compromises your perimeter network security and modifies your organization's World Wide Web home page to include sarcastic comments on the quality of security at your site, and that page is in turn seen by many of your customers? What is the damage to your organization's reputation? Will your company lose customers? It is the gray areas where management needs to focus its attention most on the effect of the possible loss on the organization's overall business.

3.4 Evaluating and Testing Your Safeguards

Once you have completed the threat assessment portion of the risk analysis, you can move on to identifying the current security controls that you have in place. A *security control* (or safeguard) is something that either prevents a potential threat or limits its potential impact. Safeguards fall into three categories: physical, administrative, and technical. Effective security relies on having all three types of safeguards.

We have discussed typical physical safeguards in section 2.1. Administrative safeguards are procedural in nature and include formalized policies and procedures; training programs such as disaster preparedness, new employee orientation, and security awareness training; and messages displayed to users when they log in (often called "logon banners") that warn intruders of the penalties for unauthorized access. Technical safeguards include monitoring and restricting network access via some means such as a firewall, restricting the use of privileged system accounts, and controlling the default permissions and ownership of files and directories.

After identifying the safeguards you have in place, you need to determine how well they are working. During this process, you need to evaluate whether the safeguards are doing the job they were intended to do and whether there are threats for which no safeguard is currently installed. Testing your safeguards can be enlightening and even fun. One approach to testing computer-related security safeguards is to use a "tiger team." We discuss this approach in section 5.3.

To test your organization's physical safeguards, have a third party who is not familiar with your site walk around the premises to see what he or she can access and to see if anyone stops to question this person. Here are some questions this procedure should answer:

- Are building access controls sufficient to keep a stranger from entering restricted areas?
- Do employees stop people they are unfamiliar with and ask to see identification?
- Are restricted rooms locked during the required hours?

■ Do your employees wear their ID badges at all times?

Procedural or administrative safeguards can be tested in several ways. One is to stage a mock security incident to see how well your staff responds. This test should answer questions such as:

■ Do you have incident response procedures in place?

■ Have you identified an "incident response team"?

■ Do team members understand their roles and responsibilities?

■ Does the incident response team know what information should be logged and tracked?

Incident response procedures are discussed in section 5.5.

Another way to test your procedural safeguards is to have a third party try various social engineering schemes. (See section 2.5 for an explanation of social engineering attacks.) For example, a person can call your organization's internal support hotline, pretending to be an important officer within the company who forgot her password. This scheme will test whether the support employees provide the password over the phone or if they attempt to verify who is calling. Another scheme is to have someone call up pretending to be a new employee who has requested an account that has not yet been installed. He asks to have the account installed and activated right away and threatens to take the issue to management if his demand is not met. This scheme is designed to test how the support staff responds under pressure. If they create the account and activate it without checking with the caller's manager, then you know there is a problem, and future training is warranted. These are just a few of many methods you can use to test your administrative safeguards.

As you go through the process of testing safeguards, every fault or weakness you find should be added to a list. At the end of the process, you can analyze the list and determine which risks are acceptable and which are not. Threats that have a low frequency rate or a low damage loss may be acceptable; the others should be corrected.

3.5 Formulating a Plan for Added Security

Ideally, you will select and implement corrective solutions that greatly reduce the risks posed by the threats you have identified. Solutions that offer only a small decrease in your risk level may not be cost-effective. By contrast, a single corrective measure may simultaneously reduce multiple risks and hence be of great value. If your vulnerability level is high in many areas and your organization does not have the resources to implement controls for the entire facility, then prioritize your areas of concern. Systems that store and process critical or confidential information (e.g., sales and marketing data, personnel records, accounting information) should be secured before general-purpose data-processing systems. You may even need to restructure your organization's LAN so as to isolate critical departments by using internal firewalls. (See section 2.4.1.4 for a description of firewalls.) As more money becomes available, you can implement additional security measures.

Implementing an appropriate level of security costs money—in some cases, a lot of money. One of your roles as a manager is to determine the appropriate level of security and how much money should be spent to achieve it. In this section, we have examined the risk analysis process as a tool to assess threats and the costs associated with them. Armed with this information, you must decide how much security you want. The more money and resources you are willing to dedicate to achieving security, the more secure your site will be. But as with many infrastructure investments, you will reach a point of diminishing returns. The proper level of security balances your need for protection with your desire for productivity and convenience. Achieving strong security at the expense of employee productivity and morale is, in the long run, unwise.

When considering the cost of added security, it is important to maintain a sense of balance. As a wise saying puts it, "Security is economics." In other words, you can always improve site security with an increased investment, but you need to decide when such expenditures are economically sensible. A determined adversary with unlimited resources will always be able to defeat your security measures; the trick is to make it too costly for the typical would-be attacker to compromise your systems, without requiring that your organization spend a fortune. Make sure your spending on security is consistent with the cost and probability of compromise.

If your organization lacks the financial resources to invest heavily in hardware and software to implement security, do not despair. Procedural security controls such as the policies discussed in chapter 5, along with a good security awareness program, can go a great distance toward improving security. In terms of technical measures, many security tools are available for free on the Internet.

4.0 Trust Models

Before determining which security policies are needed for your organization, you should consider the issue of trust. In particular, who and what are you willing to trust? Access to resources will be provided to trusted employees and users; others will be denied such access. Among those given access, the level of access provided will likely depend to some extent on the level of trust invested in the individual. Hence, trust is a principle underlying any security policy and must be considered before security-specific policies and procedures are developed.

4.1 Who Has Access

Deciding who has access to your corporate resources may be as simple as stating that only employees have access. But this is not a workable policy for many companies and organizations; a number of special cases may apply to your site. For example, many companies will have one or more contractors working for them at a given time. These temporary employees may need access to computing resources. Likewise, support engineers working for the vendors who supply your computing equipment may need access to some of that equipment in order to provide support and maintenance service. This is true both when the support engineers work onsite, and are treated essentially as employees, and when they need to perform remote diagnostics on your organization's equipment. Finally, if your organization is conducting codevelopment or research with other organizations, members of those organizations may need access to some of your computing resources.

The safest way to approach the problem of determining who receives access to your organization's computer systems is to use the principle of "least access," meaning that individuals are given access to the minimal set of resources (and level of access on those resources) that they need in order to perform their jobs effectively. Using this guideline, vendors who need remote access in order to perform a diagnostic test on a computer system at your facility from their office would be given an active account only on the specific machine undergoing the diagnostic and only during the period during which the remote diagnostic is being performed. Regular employees would have access to any computing resources they need in order to perform their jobs, but not to unrelated resources.

Underlying the access question is the issue of trust. Who and what is trustworthy?

4.2 The Issue of Trust

Your decisions about who and what to trust will have a major impact on the level of your organization's security. As with all security issues, the question of trust is a difficult balancing act. Place too much trust in too many people, and you lessen your level of security. Don't trust enough, and you will have a difficult time finding people who will want to work for your organization, and those who do work for you will have a hard time accomplishing their jobs. The same idea applies to machines: if you trust your equipment's security or reliability too much, you're bound to be disappointed (or worse) eventually. If you don't trust your equipment enough, you are likely to underutilize its abilities and will therefore suffer a loss in potential productivity.

Trust is something that develops over time; it does not develop instantaneously. As a manager, it's your job to set trust levels and expectations for your employees, for people who do business with your organization, and for your organization's computing resources.

4.2.1 *Trusting Resources* Deciding what resources to trust can be tricky. In an ideal world, all products and services would be completely trustworthy. Experience has shown that in this regard, a high-tech environment is far from an ideal world. For example, some system vendors continue to ship software with known security vulnerabilities. Many vendors respond with painful slowness to reports of security flaws in their products. Unfortunately, it is not safe to assume that a new hardware or software product purchased from a vendor is secure. Such products should be carefully examined by a knowledgeable system administrator before installation. This won't prevent security problems from cropping up later, but it will reduce the risk associated with misconfigured new systems.

Resources can also fail in ways that affect system availability but not security. Loss of availability means financial losses for the organization affected. These losses may be direct, such as a network failure affecting an ISP (whose main business is reselling network bandwidth to customers), or indirect, such as failure of disk drives leading to lost productivity while workers wait for files to be restored.

Unfortunately, failures are common. In the high-tech world, vendors are constantly "pushing the envelope" to deliver faster, more powerful, and more cost-effective products. A side effect of this trend is that software and hardware bugs sometimes go unnoticed during the development process due to a reduced emphasis on quality assurance and testing. As a manager, you will need to evaluate the levels of trust appropriate for the hardware and software systems in use by your organization and, where possible, to implement appropriate procedures to ensure that data loss and downtime are minimal if failures do occur.

*4.2.2 **Trusting People*** How much trust to invest in your employees poses another delicate balancing act. Too much trust opens your organization to unnecessary security risks. Not enough trust leads to resentful and/or unproductive employees.

It is sometimes wise to trust different categories of employees to different degrees. For example, regular full-time employees might be trusted more than temporary employees or independent contractors. It may be wise to withhold privileged system access from new employees until they learn about the organization's procedures (both security and otherwise), system philosophy and configuration, and the like—not because the employee is distrusted, but because a new employee with privileged access could accidentally do significant damage to systems they do not yet fully understand

Although it is outside the scope of this booklet, we briefly mention that trust extends beyond the realm of computer security. The risks of placing trust in untrustworthy employees existed long before the computer was invented. Computers haven't made people less trustworthy, but in many cases they have increased the amount of damage a disgruntled employee can do to an employer's finances and reputation.

One way to avoid making a mistake in the area of employee trust is to incorporate background checks into your hiring process. Although the appropriate degree of such checking will depend on the type of job for which an individual is applying, even simple background checking can help your organization avoid embarrassment or financial loss. We continue our discussion of hiring practices as they relate to computer security in section 5.7.

*4.2.3 **The Best Trust Model*** Three possible trust models are

Trust all users all of the time.

Trust some users some of the time.

Trust only those who must be trusted, and trust them as little as possible ("least privilege").

The most relaxed trust model dictates that anyone doing work within or with your organization is completely trusted. This trust model is the easiest to enforce because it frees you from needing to implement any internal security measures. For example, one of the authors worked for a large computer company that used a firewall to secure the company's internal network from the Internet. But the company took virtually no internal security measures to prevent employees from exceeding the privileges necessary to do their jobs. Many accounts, including some privileged administrator accounts, had no passwords. Most machines had an anonymous, passwordless "guest" account that allowed anyone in the organization to login to any such computer, with virtually no audit trail. Most employees liked this policy because no security restrictions interfered with their ability to do their work and to share their machines and data. The organization had a strong culture of employees trusting each other, so it was felt that this was a workable security policy.

The "trust all the people all of the time" trust model usually starts when an organization is small and never changes. For a small start-up company, this may be an appropriate trust model. But for a large organization with thousands of employees and many remote offices, it is not a wise choice. The problem with a trust model this relaxed is that one bad apple can ruin the entire company's security. This "bad apple" can be a human or a technical vulnerability—or both. For example, the company discussed previously allowed any employee to dial in to the company's computer network. Access to the network required only a per-user reusable password. If an employee were to write down and subsequently lose in public the phone number of the company's dial-in modem pool, along with his or her username and password, a malicious individual could dial in and, once on the internal network, wreak havoc on virtually every machine in the company.

Unfortunately, studies show that the majority of computer crime is committed by insiders. The Computer Security Institute's 1996 Computer Crime and Security Survey reports that over 50% of the respondents who said they had experienced an intrusion were able to trace the incident to an employee on the inside. In such a world, unconditional trust of employees is trust misplaced.

The opposite of trusting all the people all of the time is a "least privilege" philosophy. This trust model dictates that administrators give users access to the least amount of resources and data necessary for users to do their respective jobs. Such a model is probably inappropriate for most sites. One might envision a highly classified facility where this model might be appropriate. In such a protected environment, many technical controls would be implemented to ensure that employees cannot access or modify information or files to which they have not explicitly been given clearance. The US Government's "Orange Book," discussed in chapter 6, presents guidelines for designing, building, and running systems for this sort of environment.

The most appropriate trust model for most facilities follows the "trust some of the people some of the time" philosophy. This does not mean that employees should be untrusted, but rather that management should exercise caution when providing employees with access to information and other valuable company resources. In this trust environment, people will acquire access to the resources that they need to accomplish their work or that they feel will assist their productivity. Privileged system access and access to hardware and software supplies are given out only to those who can justify such access. Technical controls, such as access logging, are put in place to ensure people do not violate the trust model. Employees are typically required to justify requests for remote access and home equipment and may even be required to sign a document stating they will abide by certain rules and guidelines. The monitoring needed to enforce this trust model is similar to that needed to enforce "least privilege," but this trust model is more relaxed in its criteria for granting access to information and systems.

An organization that uses the "trust some of the people some of the time" trust model may decide to isolate sensitive information from all but those who can prove they need access to it. For example, personnel records would be available only to individuals in the personnel department and sales and financial information only to those in the sales department or in upper management. This can be accomplished by isolating the systems where the information resides or by isolating the network for the department whose information is to be protected. Internal firewalls can be useful in this case.

No matter which trust model you decide to employ at your facility, you must remain aware of the risks facing your organization and, when necessary, re-evaluate the trust model you have adopted. What may be successful and appropriate this year may be completely inappropriate next year.

5.0 Security Policies and Procedures: The Roadmap

Once you've identified the threats your organization faces and the security measures appropriate for addressing them, it's time to write the necessary security policies and procedures. These important documents will serve as the foundation of your security infrastructure.

5.1 Security Policies

Security policies are among the most crucial elements of a security infrastructure. Unfortunately, the security policy design phase is often the most difficult part of implementing good security. Developing these policies is a process that will involve a joint effort among management staff, who will need to enforce the policies, and employees, who are expected to adhere to the policies. These people must work together as a team to create a series of guidelines that everyone can understand and by which all users are willing to abide.

There are three key elements to consider in the policy design and implementation phase:

1. How specific should the policy be?

2. How much control should the policy enforce?

3. What is the appropriate security policy structure?

Security policies are not meant to be detailed technical implementation plans. Policies that are too specific are likely to be inflexible as well as difficult for the user community to understand. But a policy that is too general will be of minimal usefulness. The policy should be specific to the point of describing what is to be protected and why, but without specifying a particular method of implementation.

Security policies must balance protection with their impact on productivity. Policies that hinder employee productivity, or impose controls that don't seem reasonable to employees, are unlikely to be followed. Furthermore, if an oppressive security policy is implemented via technical means, employees are likely to become creative in finding ways to subvert the enforcement mechanisms. Your organization's security needs and culture will largely dictate what balance is most comfortable for all involved.

Formulating a security policy structure is highly dependent on an organization's specific circumstances. There are a number of areas that should be covered by security policies and several ways in which the task can be approached. Some sites choose to place all policy-related documents into a single large site security policy. Many organizations have found the following separate policies, at a minimum, to be useful:

acceptable use policy—discusses and defines appropriate use of the organization's computing resources

user account policy—outlines requirements for individuals who request and maintain accounts on the organization's computer systems

remote access policy —defines the acceptable methods of remotely connecting to the organization's LAN

information protection policy—discusses how the organization's information is protected from unauthorized access, inadvertent disclosure, or loss

network connection policy—establishes rules for the addition of new devices to the organization's network

special access policy—specifies rules regarding use of privileged system accounts

For a more detailed discussion of the policy design process, we refer you to *A Guide to Developing Computing Policy Documents,* edited by by Barbara L. Dijker (USENIX Association, 1996).

5.2 Policy Implementors

One attractive feature of a security policy is that once management finalizes it, system administrators can implement it largely on their own. Ideally, when confronted with a security implementation decision, system administrators can simply refer to the security policy for guidance and can determine without management intervention the security technology that is best suited to implementing the policy's requirements. In practice, certain real-world constraints may occasionally require further decisions from management (e.g., "How much money are we willing to spend on hardware tokens for authentication of users accessing the organization's network remotely?"). Still, the security policy should offer enough guidance for the technical staff to decide on their own most issues of a purely technical nature (e.g., "Should we allow service X through our firewall?" "Which vendor's security product best suits our organization's needs?").

Large organizations should ensure that all system administrators' actions are coordinated. Your security is only as strong as the weakest link in the chain; if you have several departments independently establish security measures without central coordination, some departments are likely to have weaker protection than others, leaving your overall organization victim to the weaknesses of the least protected department. Therefore, if your organization uses a different group of system administrators for each department, it is wise to designate one or a few system administrators to coordinate security measures across the entire organization. If you use a firewall, it is best to have at most a few security gurus who are solely responsible for all firewall operations. Finally, consider establishing a procedure for dissemination of organization wide security advisories; the corporate security department, if you have one, might wish to take responsibility for this task. Over the past few years many companies have decided to hire or specify one employee as a "corporate computer security officer," responsible for planning security measures and supervising their implementation and maintenance. Having a separate security officer ensures that security responsibilities are not handed exclusively to system administrators, who may not have time to devote the necessary attention to this important issue.

5.3 Reviewing the Policy Implementation

A security policy is not much use if its implementation is faulty or inadequate. Periodic reviews are helpful. The reviewer(s) should examine security-relevant decisions made by system administrators in order to verify that those decisions were appropriate. Often it is best for these reviews to be conducted by an independent third party, so that the review can take place without the distorting effect of office politics. You may have the choice between an outside consultant or an internal security expert; both options have fairly obvious advantages and disadvantages.

In some environments, corporate auditors might require a formal audit of your security provisions. Your organization may also have certain legal responsibilities. For example, publicly traded corporations are required to meet a good-faith "due diligence" standard; your legal department may want to verify compliance with this requirement by performing a security audit.

There exist a variety of tools that can test your system for vulnerabilities to the most common security loopholes. Your system administrator(s) is the best source for information about such tools.

Another approach to evaluating the effectiveness of your security measures is to perform penetration testing. "Tiger teams," experts in penetration testing, can be hired to attempt to break into your system under carefully controlled conditions. The value of tiger teams is somewhat controversial. One advantage of tiger teams is that because their members are not employees of your organization, their analysis is not constrained by preconceptions about your company's procedures and policies. Also, tiger teams typically use toolkits (collections of software programs that perform a set of related tasks) to automatically scan for the latest and most common vulnerabilities. However, a tiger team may not be worth the cost, given your environment; if your organization's computer resources and security requirements are fairly simple, penetration testing by a tiger team may be overkill.

One of the most difficult parts of ensuring the appropriateness of your security implementation is simply keeping it up to date. The Internet is changing at an incredibly rapid pace, and at least every few years major alterations occur that require a complete re-evaluation of your security approach. On a more day-to-day basis, regular maintenance of site security will be necessary as new vulnerabilities become known and as users demand access to new services. To this end, system administrators should be encouraged to stay current with the latest information about computer security. They also must be provided with the resources they need to ensure that your organization's security implementation remains adequate and in keeping with the goals of your security policy.

We present some additional methods for maintaining your security infrastructure in section 7.2, and appendix B lists a number of resources that can help managers and administrators stay current in the area of security. Besides written resources, conferences and workshops are very valuable ways to stay up to date and to network with other professionals in the computer security field. Professional contacts are often the most valuable source of information available, so it is worth sending someone from your organization to important security conferences and to meetings of local computer security interest groups.

5.4 Assurance

After investing in resources to implement your security policy, you will want to know that the measures will work as desired and will keep working. This robustness quality is known as *assurance*.

Overlooking the assurance level of security measures by focusing only on their functionality is a grave error. Indeed, some environments may require exceptionally high levels of assurance rather than fancy security controls. Even if your security requirements are very simple, they may need to work no matter what. (For example, assurance is clearly of utmost importance in the security policy "absolutely don't let the toxic radioactive waste escape from its container at any time"!)

Functionality and assurance do not go hand in hand. If anything, more sophisticated features tend to come at the expense of assurance. Fancy functionality usually implies complexity, and with complexity inevitably comes unexpected and long-undiscovered security loopholes. Programmers and managers must face the fact that it is essentially impossible to write large, bug-free programs. Fortunately, there are several techniques that can be applied to increase the level of assurance afforded by security systems.

One popular technique for improving assurance asks implementors to apply standard techniques from software engineering. At first, it may seem odd to apply methods used in software programming to the design and implementation of a policy. But further thought shows the value of this approach: much wisdom from software engineering is concerned with the organization and maintenance of large systems, and those are exactly the problems faced in designing and implementing a security policy. Useful rules of thumb from the experience of software engineering include the following:

- Strive for security through extreme simplicity—complex systems are difficult to analyze and are prone to errors.
- Keep implementations modular—reuse proven solutions whenever possible.
- Carefully explore your assumptions and their consequences.
- Maintain a history of mistakes and how they were fixed. Periodically scan this list looking for patterns and weak points in the system that need improvement. Document this process and its results.
- Be conservative.

There are a few rules of thumb that the security community has found especially helpful:

- Prepare for parts of the system to fail unexpectedly.
- Avoid single points of failure.
- Apply multiple levels of protection liberally–don't depend on any one protection mechanism, but instead implement multiple mechanisms that back each other up. For example, you might use discretionary access controls to prevent unauthorized access to certain confidential files, and then back that up with file encryption "just in case."
- Take advantage of diversity of defenses, where possible, because very different mechanisms are less likely to fail simultaneously. For example, you might implement a perimeter defense but still install intrusion detection systems in your internal network in case the perimeter is compromised. As another example, you will probably want to back up your technical defenses with social enforcement measures.
- Be aware of the principle of least privilege: grant employees the least amount of privilege they legitimately need to perform their duties.
- Make your system fail-safe. That is, if your system must fail, it should fail in a way that denies access to adversaries, rather than failing in a way that leave your system open to attack. For example, a fail-safe firewall might completely shut down all Internet access if it fails. This way you know an intruder won't be able to get into your network upon such a failure, and you receive the added benefit that a failure is likely to be noticed very quickly!

- By default, deny everything not expressly allowed—and be conservative in what you allow.

- Your system is only as secure as its weakest link; therefore, it often makes sense to establish a central "choke point" (e.g., a firewall) where all security-critical decisions can be made.

- It is notoriously difficult to secure a system against insider attack, so make sure your users understand the reasons behind your security measures and are willing to follow them. Also, be very certain that your security implementors are trustworthy.

Another important method for improving assurance is quality control. When your security system is initially designed and implemented, call for a peer review of the system. Have someone who was not intimately involved in the policy-drafting process look at your work and check it for mistakes. If you have a lot of trouble explaining your policy or your implementation to a newcomer, then your approach is probably too complex to be very secure. Once the system is up and running, you can run penetration tests to make sure that it operates as expected.

Organizations with extremely high assurance requirements might want to apply formal methods to verify the correctness of their design and implementation. Unfortunately, formal methods are not yet practical for everyday use; they are appropriate only for the most demanding circumstances. Organizations with extremely high assurance requirements should also consider using systems that have been evaluated by the US Government's Trusted Product Evaluation Program (TPEP). This program is described in section 6.3.

We do not mean to suggest that you adopt an attitude of complete paranoia toward the issue of assurance. But assurance is often viewed as secondary in importance to security functionality, and that misprioritization can lead to a system that fails despite the best of intentions.

5.5 Incident Preparedness and Response

We have discussed many facets of computer security, including the threats organizations face and possible responses to them. But regardless of how many security precautions an organization takes, it is likely eventually to experience a security incident. This section provides some suggestions about how to respond to such incidents.

We make a distinction here between an "incident" and a "disaster." An incident is a small-scale event that adversely affects some of an organization's computing resources in a small way. Examples include intruders and viruses. A disaster is a large-scale event such as a fire, earthquake, or flood that causes a major disruption to some or all computing facilities.

5.5.1 Formulating an Incident Response Procedure Every site should formulate an incident response procedure that outlines the roles and responsibilities of staff members in the event that the organization must respond to a computer security incident. The incident response process can be divided into seven stages:

1. isolating the system or network where the problem occurred

2. identifying the problem (Is it an active intruder on the system or a security flaw that was exploited weeks ago and is just now coming to light?)

3. containing the problem to protect as yet unaffected resources

4. terminating the attack, if it or any actions that it initiated are still in progress

5. eradicating the fundamental vulnerability that was exploited in order to protect against future attacks

6. recovering normal function of facilities

7. performing a follow-up analysis

The incident response procedure defines the areas of responsibility for the response team members. The number of people involved in responding to an incident will vary according to the size and scope of the incident. In many cases, the security analyst or system administrator may be the "team." Regardless of the team's size, it is important for the procedure to outline who has what responsibilities, such as who will inform management, who will log important events, and who will interview relevant personnel.

The response procedure outlines the steps to be taken during and following a security incident. An important general guideline is to thoroughly document all information related to an incident and all actions taken in response to it. The implications and extent of a security incident are not always known at the onset, so documentation even of details that may not seem immediately relevant can prove useful later on.

Proper evidence handling, particularly careful preservation of evidence, is important if you intend to prosecute the individual(s) who caused an incident. Before any files or other traces left behind by an intruder are moved, the affected systems should be backed up and relevant text files (e.g., audit logs) printed out on paper. Laws regarding evidence preservation and tracking vary from jurisdiction to jurisdiction, but you have the best chance of having your evidence accepted by a court if you can prove there is no way it could have been tampered with or otherwise corrupted. We suggest that you contact a local law enforcement agency to learn about the evidence rules that pertain to your area.

The incident response procedure should include a discussion of who will be informed about different classes of incidents. Possibilities include CERT (see section B.1.2 for contact information), the FBI, vendors of the affected hardware or software, the affected organization's management, the affected organization's computer system users, and system administrators within and possibly outside of the affected organization.

The issue of who to notify is a controversial one. Companies are often reluctant to tell anyone about a security incident for fear of generating negative press. The company's customers could lose faith in the organization's products, and stockholders might become worried that management doesn't have a handle on security issues. Some organizations won't even tell their own users about security incidents for fear of encouraging users to try to find and exploit related or unrelated flaws. And if information about an incident leaks from the affected organization during the investigation phase, successful prosecution of individuals involved in the incident may become more difficult.

If an organization wishes to disseminate information regarding an incident, a single individual in the organization should be designated as the point of contact, and the information released should first be reviewed by management. Although it may seem that releasing information about a security incident is a lose-lose situation, this is not the case. A vulnerability that affects one organization (e.g., a security hole in a widely used program) is likely to affect many others. Only if information about security vulnerabilities is promulgated throughout technical communities can there ever be hope of correcting these problems on a widespread basis. Because the nature of most organizations is to protect themselves first and to worry about the rest of the world second, many computer security incidents are never publicized outside the affected organizations.

It is not feasible to describe the exact procedures that should be followed in response to every imaginable type of security incident. Instead, try to categorize potential incidents into four broad categories:

1. viruses and worms (described in section 2.3.5)

2. security probes from the Internet (e.g., an attempted login connection from an unauthorized individual or an attempt to exercise a program bug)

3. intrusion from the Internet (a successful compromise in which the intruder gains system access)

4. security violations originating from within your organization

Then, for each category, describe the general guidelines to be followed in response to an incident of that type.

Once the incident response procedure is written and approved, your organization should test it by staging a mock incident and seeing how well the relevant employees respond. This exercise may bring to light flaws in the procedure or additional areas of incident response that need to be covered.

5.5.2 A Sample Scenario This section presents a general computer security incident scenario. In particular, we detail actions to be taken that correspond to the seven-step process described in section 5.5.1. Most computer security incidents are discovered when a system or network is not responding the way it does normally or a user or system administrator detects signs that someone has "visited" the site. (As an example of the latter, in August, 1996, hackers replaced the US Department of Justice's World Wide Web home page with one of their own making. The attack was quite obvious to anyone who looked at the page.)

First, upon detecting that an attack has occurred or is in progress, you should isolate the affected system(s) and/or network segment(s), in order to contain the problem. If someone is actively launching an attack from the Internet, you may want to temporarily disconnect your site from the Internet.

Second, identify the problem. This will involve looking at system configuration files to see if they have changed, determining whether important system programs have been deleted or modified, and checking for undesirable programs such as network sniffers that may have been installed by the intruder. The process used to identify the problem is often referred to as *incident forensics* and is a growing field in the computer security realm. Only once you have identified the problem and the full extent of any damage will you know how to proceed.

Third, you need to contain the problem. In some cases, it may be "self-contained" to the host that was compromised. In the event of a virus infection, you need to stop the spread of the virus by running virus eradication software on all affected hosts. If the problem is a network sniffer, you need to disable the sniffer program and remove the sniffer log file so that intruders cannot access the information logged by the sniffer.

If the problem is an active intruder on the system, two approaches may be taken. The safest approach is to remove all processes corresponding to programs the intruder is running, to destroy any files the intruder has created, and to restore to their original condition any files that the intruder has deleted or modified. A riskier approach is to isolate from the rest of your network the system that the intruder is using and to simply observe what the intruder does. Clearly, this course of action should be taken only by a very knowledgeable system administrator. Though it is somewhat risky, this approach provides the possibility that the intruder may reveal, while being observed, information about other systems (possibly at your facility) he or she has attacked in the past or clues to his or her identity. You may also be able to learn more about the vulnerabilities the intruder is exploiting if you watch this person in action.

Fourth, you need to eradicate the problem and take steps to ensure that it does not recur. In the case of a virus, you should install antivirus software throughout your organization. (You should already be running such software, but for some companies, a virus infestation prompts management to think about virus protection for the first time.) For operating system vulnerabilities, you should contact the operating system vendor for a patch. If no patch is yet available for the vulnerability, you may be able to temporarily disable the vulnerable operating system program. In some cases, preventing recurrence of a particular attack may require fundamentally rethinking your security philosophy and policies. You may decide that you erred on the side of convenience or expense in weighing the security versus convenience equation.

Fifth, you should restore the affected systems to their normal operating state. This may require reinstalling software from a trusted source to ensure that any programs modified or deleted by the attacker have been restored to their original version. This phase will most likely require restoration of data that were stored on the affected systems.

Sometimes it is difficult to determine when an attack actually began. Some viruses are so good at "hiding" that they may not be noticed until many months after they first entered your system. Do not make the mistake of blindly recovering programs from the latest backup, especially in the case of PC software that resided on a virus-infected PC—you could simply be replacing an infected program with an older, but also infected, copy of the same program. This is why we suggest that the operating system and application programs be reinstalled from their original media rather than from backup tapes. Assuming the original media are read-only, you can be assured that they were not affected by the security incident.

Sixth, you will want to re-enable connectivity to the Internet or other networks from which you may have disconnected your site during the initial incident response.

Finally, the incident response team should perform a postmortem analysis on the incident. This process is key to improving response and recovery from future incidents. Each person who was involved in the response process should participate. During this phase, some important questions include:

Why did the incident occur?

Was there a breakdown in a security control?

Was the incident the result of carelessness on someone's part?

Was it the result of a threat no one had considered?

Did members of the incident response team know who they were?

Did the incident team know what actions to take?

Did the incident team know who to call for additional assistance?

Depending on the source or cause of the incident, you may want to re-evaluate your security controls and/or provide additional training to your support staff. During the postmortem analysis, the incident response team should discuss how well (or poorly) they felt the incident response was handled and should recommend changes to the process. The postmortem analysis is a valuable learning tool that can reduce the likelihood of future incidents, limit the damage of any future incidents that do occur, and improve your organization's incident response process and policy.

5.6 Disaster Planning and Recovery

Incident response procedures should be sufficient to handle small-scale problems such as an intruder's attack on a few machines. But response to a large-scale disruption, such as a major power outage or earthquake, calls for a disaster recovery plan. Disaster planning is often neglected by organizations, perhaps because (fortunately!) disasters do not occur frequently. If a long-term (e.g., more than 48-hour) disruption of computing resources would cause a major financial loss to your organization, then a disaster plan is essential to the ongoing success of your business. Even if such is not the case, you still need a plan to guide recovery from a disaster that permanently or temporarily disables some or all of your computing equipment.

We use the term "disaster" to denote an event that causes the loss of critical system components. Examples of disasters include the following:

a major earthquake that damages buildings

destruction of a building due to a major fire or explosion

a power outage that lasts more than two days

flooding in computer rooms due to heavy rains or a broken water main

In this section, we provide an overview of the important issues to consider when formulating a disaster plan for your site. An extended discussion is beyond the scope of this booklet. However, a number of books and tutorials discuss the process. Some books on disaster recovery and planning are: Arnold, Richard. *Disaster Recovery Plan.* (New York: John Wiley & Sons, 1993); and Meyers, Kenneth. *Total Contingency Planning for Disasters.* (New York: John Wiley & Sons, 1996). Additionally, various consulting companies specialize in disaster planning and recovery.

The main component of a disaster plan is an outline of what must be done to keep critical business resources running after a disaster. The major goals of the plan are to minimize the impact of the disaster on the organization's ability to do business and to expedite the organization's return to normal operating conditions. The disaster response and recovery process can be divided into the following phases:

- onset of the disaster
- response by on-site personnel
- damage and impact assessment and analysis
- transition to emergency operating mode
- restoration of normal business operations

Before you can begin to formulate a disaster response plan, you must determine which resources are critical to the survival of your organization during an extended outage. This process should involve the appropriate levels of upper management, with uniform agreement as the end result. Also needed is an understanding of the possible disasters that might occur and how they would affect your business capability. In chapter 3, we discussed the risk analysis process, which provides a detailed analysis of risks and threats; and in chapter 2, we examined some of the physical threats that can cause a disaster, along with some technical methods that can be used to mitigate a disaster's effects.

Disasters usually occur without warning. During the onset of a disaster, your primary goal is to ensure the safety of everyone in the immediate disaster area. Where appropriate, people should evacuate the affected facilities. Individuals designated as members of the disaster response team should know where to report after a disaster and how to contact other members of the team. Given the general pandemonium that naturally occurs during a major disaster, your written disaster plan should be easily accessible and already familiar to those who must implement it. If the only copy is stored on a hard drive that has been incinerated, the plan won't do you much good. This rule applies to any sort of emergency response document, such as the emergency contact list—there should be many copies, both electronic and on paper, and they should be readily available. Copies should be stored offsite as well as onsite.

Individuals' reactions in the face of a disaster will vary. Some will remain calm and attentive; others will become dazed and panic stricken. Your disaster plan should take into account the possibility that some response team members may be physically or psychologically unable to perform their duties.

The response plan should provide a method to calculate the impact and damage of the disaster. This is important because the results can be used to determine which emergency operating mode is put into effect. A thorough disaster plan will outline several emergency operating modes based on the severity of damage. The severity of damage will determine how much the organization's operations are affected, which in turn will determine how much money the organization will lose each day its computer facilities remain affected.

Based on the impact a disaster might have on an organization's ability to do business, management may wish to maintain an emergency operating facility that can be used for computer operations until the disaster damage is repaired. Such alternate sites are often referred to as "hot" and "cold" sites. A *hot site* is an alternate facility that is equipped with all the necessary hardware, software, and wiring for the business to move its operations there on short notice. In the event of a major loss of computing resources, employees are relocated to the hot site along with backups of critical software and data. A *cold site* is also an alternate business location, but it is essentially an empty building equipped only with the proper electrical and communication infrastructure to support business relocation to that site. In the event of a major disaster, the organization would need to procure the computers and other equipment necessary to resume its data-processing operations at the cold site.

Once the transition to an emergency operating mode has been completed, the restoration process can begin. Depending on the extent of damage, this could be a long, involved process requiring that facilities be rebuilt, new equipment be procured and installed, etc. The restoration process should include a postmortem analysis of the organization's response to the disaster. Members of the response team and other appropriate personnel should meet to discuss how well the plan worked and what changes should be made to improve the process in the event of a future disaster.

Regardless of the complexity of an organization's disaster plan, annual disaster drills should be conducted to test the effectiveness and thoroughness of the plan. It is difficult to predict what will happen in a disaster, but rehearsal can help to identify the more obvious procedural errors.

Formulating and implementing a disaster response and recovery plan is not a single task, but rather a continual process. Organizations are rarely static in either size or structure. A plan written one year may become totally inappropriate the next. A successful disaster response plan will be fully tested on an annual basis and revised as necessary—sometimes in the aftermath of a disaster.

5.7 Hiring Practices

In chapter 4 we mentioned that most computer crime is the result of insider attacks. But the risk from employee-related threats can be minimized to some extent by taking appropriate security precautions during the hiring process. For example, you may decide to do the following:

- screen resumes for "red flags" such as references to hacker activity

- perform reference checks

- perform background checks

- require new hires to sign an agreement form outlining the company's expectations with respect to employee adherence to computer security guidelines

- provide security awareness training as part of new employee orientation

5.8 Computer Security and the Law

As a manager, you need to be aware of and understand the legal aspects of computer security. This field is undergoing constant change. Although computer crime existed before the general public had access to the Internet, the number of crimes involving computers is increasing as the number of computers and users on the Internet increase. Law enforcement agencies have not been able to keep up with the rate of increase, and many feel that the government has not responded quickly enough in writing new federal laws governing computer crime. But laws related to computer crime do exist. If you are significantly concerned about computer-related crime or foresee the possibility of one day needing to prosecute someone for such crimes, we suggest you contact a lawyer who is versed the relevant laws.

For a layman's discussion of these laws, we refer you to Icove, David; Seger, Karl; and VonStorch, William. *Computer Crime: A Crimefighter's Handbook.* (Sebastopol, CA: O'Reilly & Associates, 1995).

Deciding if and when to involve the authorities during or after a computer security incident is an important question with which managers must grapple. A number of issues, such as jurisdictions and the impact of the crime, should be considered before "calling the police." In many cases, incident response organizations such as CERT (see appendix B) can help you make the determination of whether to involve law enforcement, but they may not be able to respond quickly enough for your needs. Our advice is to consult your organization's legal department or to seek outside legal advice before you decide to inform, or not to inform, law enforcement following a computer security incident.

6.0 The Orange Book

You can't read much about computer security without eventually coming across a reference to the "Orange Book." The Orange Book is the common name for the US Department of Defense's Trusted Computer Security Evaluation Criteria, a document that defines levels of computer security protection and assurance. The trustworthiness of a system is summarized by placing it into one of seven categories. In order of increasing security, these categories are D, C1, C2, B1, B2, B3, and A1. (Category D describes "systems that have been evaluated but that fail to meet the requirements for a higher evaluation class" —in other words, systems that do not meet the requirements for even the lowest meaningful rating level).

In this section, we provide not a detailed summary of the Orange Book—which is itself not a very long document—but rather an overview of some of the security concepts and requirements typical of the Orange Book. Most commercial operating systems not designed for use by the government are never submitted to the government for evaluation. But even though these guidelines were designed primarily to protect US government computer systems, the concepts involved are relevant to any computer security effort.

6.1 Terminology

The Orange Book divides its recommendations into three "control objectives"—areas of computer security about which the document provides guidelines. These areas are security policy, accountability, and assurance. A *security policy* is defined as "a statement of intent with regard to control over access to and dissemination of information." *Accountability* requires that the system "assure individual accountability" whenever a security policy is invoked and that there exist the ability "for an authorized and competent agent to access and evaluate accountability information by a secure means, within a reasonable amount of time, and without undue difficulty." *Assurance* requires that the system be "designed to guarantee correct and accurate interpretation of the security policy" without "distort[ing] the intent of that policy" and that this assurance exist throughout the life of the system.

6.2 Orange Book Requirements

The Orange Book places requirements on systems in the areas of security policy (and its implementation), accountability, assurance, and documentation. In this discussion, *subject* denotes an actor, e.g., an individual or a program acting on behalf of an individual, and *object* denotes something acted upon, such as a file, a printer, or a network interface.

6.2.1 Security Policy The Orange Book addresses four aspects of security policy: discretionary access control, mandatory access control, labelling, and object reuse.

Discretionary access control is the access control mechanism found on most modern computer workstations and servers: the system distinguishes among individual users (and/or groups of users); permission to access a particular object can be limited to certain users (and/or groups of users). Only authorized individuals (usually the owner of an object and the system administrator) are allowed to change the permissions on an object. Systems rated C2 or higher must offer discretionary access control that is "capable of including or excluding access to the granularity of a single user." Systems rated B3 or A1 must use a discretionary access control mechanism that can specify, for each object, the users and groups of users allowed access to that object, as well as the access modes (e.g., read, write, or read/write) each such user or group is permitted. The access control mechanism in B3 and A1 systems must also allow specification of individuals and groups of individuals who are explicitly *denied* access to an object. These requirements are usually met by the use of an Access Control List (ACL) associated with each object.

To explain mandatory access control, we must first describe labelling. The concept of sensitivity labels is closely tied to the military notion of access levels, e.g., "unclassified," "confidential," "secret," or "top secret." A sensitivity label consists of an access level and one or more nonhierarchical categories; for example, a sensitivity label might read [SECRET, UFO-RESEARCH]. The motivation for the access level is to prevent subjects with a particular clearance level (theoretically corresponding to the individual's trustworthiness) from reading information labelled with a higher access level (they are not trusted enough to read that information) and from writing information into an object labelled with a lower access level (information obtained at the subject's current level is too sensitive to be written into that object). The nonhierarchical categories are designed to segregate information at a particular access level into compartments, so as to limit the range of information individuals can read within their own access level.

Labelling requirements begin at B1: a sensitivity label must be associated with every subject and storage object. Unlabeled data must be given labels by authorized users at the time the data are imported into the system. Additional rules specify requirements related to label integrity, exportation of labelled data out of the system (e.g., to a printer or a network), and labelling of human-readable output. Mandatory access control is the use of labels to make access decisions. All subjects and objects are assigned sensitivity labels, and the rules governing access decisions are as described previously. Requirements for mandatory access controls begin at level B1.

Finally, rules governing object reuse begin at level C2 and remain unchanged for higher security levels. The rules for object reuse require that a storage object that has been freed must be cleared of its old contents, and any previous authorizations to read the object must be deleted, before the object is reused. For example, after a file is deleted, there must be no way to access the information previously stored in the disk blocks that composed the deleted file.

6.2.2 Accountability, Assurance, and Documentation The Orange Book places additional requirements on systems in the areas of accountability, assurance, and documentation. The requirements in each area vary with the evaluation level; here we present only an overview of the types of requirements in each category. *Accountability* relates to how users identify themselves to a system (e.g., how a user logs in, and how password information is protected) and what sort of audit logs must be maintained by the system. *Assurance* refers to those aspects of a system that ensure the system correctly enforces the security policy. Assurance has both "operational" components (e.g., how the operating system prevents one executing program from interfering with another executing program) and "life-cycle" components (e.g., how a system must be tested and distributed). Finally, the documentation guidelines require four documents to be distributed with a system: the Security Features User's Guide (describing the security features of the system), the Trusted Facility Manual (rules that must be followed by the facility employing the trusted computer system), test documentation (describing how the system's security was tested by the designers), and design documentation (describing the protection philosophy and the inner workings of the mechanisms used to implement that philosophy).

6.3 The Trusted Product Evaluation Program

A computer system manufacturer wanting its system to be evaluated by the government according to the Orange Book guidelines submits the product to the Trusted Product Evaluation Program, an organizational unit within the US government's

National Security Agency. Orange Book evaluations are notorious for the length of time they take; combined with the speed at which computer technology changes, this unfortunately means that evaluated systems are often not "state of the art."

TPEP evaluates products other than operating systems. For example, the program evaluates network products (using the Trusted Network Interpretation, a set of guidelines for interpreting the TCSEC criteria in a network context), database systems (using the Trusted Database Interpretation, a set of guidelines for interpreting the TCSEC criteria in the context of a database system running on a trusted computer system), and standalone products such as biometric authentication devices (using the Computer Security Subsystem Interpretation of TCSEC). The TPEP home page is located at *<http://www.radium.ncsc.mil/tpep/>*.

6.4 Obtaining More Information

The Orange Book evaluation criteria, the associated interpretation criteria, and information on other computer security topics such as password selection are published as separate documents in the "Rainbow Series," so named because each document has a cover of a different color. The entire Rainbow Series of documents is available from:

INFOSEC Awareness Division
ATTN: X711/IAOC
Fort George G. Meade, MD 20755-6000

The TPEP recently began issuing a FAQ (Frequently Asked Questions, and answers) document related to the program. The FAQ is distributed via the USENET newsgroup *<comp.security.unix>* and is also available on FTP servers that carry the USENET newsgroup FAQs. One source is *<ftp://rtfm.mit.edu/pub/usenet-by-group/comp.security.unix /Computer_Security_Evaluation_FAQ,_Version_x.y>*, where *x.y* is the version number.

6.5 Using the Orange Book to Your Advantage

If your company produces hardware or software for use by certain government agencies, those products will have to follow the Orange Book guidelines. Conversely, if your organization's security needs are extremely strong, then it may be worthwhile to consider using only TPEP-evaluated products for your sensitive data-processing activities. Unlike TEMPEST-evaluated equipment, TPEP-evaluated equipment can be purchased by organizations not affiliated with the government. Unfortunately, TPEP-evaluated products generally cost significantly more than their unevaluated counterparts (it is costly for a company to prepare a product for submission to the evaluation process and to follow the evaluation through to completion). Because of the length of the evaluation process, evaluated products are likely to be at least one generation behind the "state of the art." Also, the cost and length of the evaluation process is greater for B2-, B3-, and A1-rated products than for B1- and C2-rated products. So as with all security decisions, the buyer must trade off cost for increased assurance.

We offer one final caveat. The standard versions of many popular UNIX variants, such as Sun's Solaris and SGI's Irix, offer "C2 features." This means that such systems can be configured to offer greater than the default level of security, but that the product does not meet the requirements of, or has not been submitted for review at, the C2 security level. Do not confuse such products with actual C2-rated systems. As of this writing, no major UNIX operating system is available at the C2 level. But DEC, HP, Harris Computer, and Silicon Graphics offer B1-rated versions of their UNIX operating systems.

7.0 Putting It All Altogether

We have discussed many facets of computer security in this booklet, with the hope of motivating management personnel to take a more proactive stance toward the issue. In almost every section, we have used intensifiers like "extremely," "crucial," and "critical" to describe the importance of the various pieces that go into a security infrastructure. We did not do this in order to overinflate the importance of security, but rather to emphasize the true importance of computer security to the success of any business or organization. All the topics we discussed are almost equally important to the whole picture—leave one out, and your security framework is incomplete.

Computer security is not something you can buy, nor is it something you can do once and then forget about. Implementing security is an ongoing process in which your goals and techniques will change as your organization evolves. Now that you have an increased awareness and understanding of what goes into building a successful security framework, we turn our discussion to how to integrate the pieces of the security puzzle in order to ensure the continued success of your security policy and implementation.

7.1 Where Should You Begin?

If you are just beginning work on a security framework, you should first assess the security philosophy of your organization. This philosophy will largely determine the importance of security for your organization. If individuals above you in the management hierarchy don't see the same need for security as you do, then your first job will be to convince them that additional security controls are needed for the good of the organization. Next, whether you are planning a new security framework or re-evaluating your organization's existing one, you should go through the risk analysis process described in chapter 3 to improve your understanding of the assets you need to protect and the existing threats to those assets. The risk analysis process will help you determine what security controls are needed.

Next you should examine what security policies have already been implemented at your site and determine their level of effectiveness. Using that information and the information presented in section 5.1 regarding the security policy design and implementation process, decide what new policies should be added. Your organization's security policies are vital because they outline administrative controls and serve as a roadmap for building the necessary technical and physical security controls. If your organization currently has few or no security policies, we suggest you review *A Guide to Developing Computing Policy Documents*, edited by Barbara L. Dijker (USENIX Association, 1996).

7.2 Maintaining Your Security Framework

Maintaining your security framework involves various tasks, most of which should be performed by your technical support staff of system administrators and security analysts. As a manager, your primary function in the continued success of your organization's security framework will involve:

- maintaining a qualified technical staff

- ensuring the technical staff has the time and resources to accomplish their work

- providing continual support for and advocacy of your security policies

- providing support for recommendations submitted by your technical staff

7.2.1 Security Audits and Audit Trail Accumulation Two critical parts of ensuring the ongoing success of your computer security implementation are security audits and audit trail accumulation. Several times throughout this booklet we have referred to the importance of these functions. As a manager, you should dedicate appropriate resources to allow system support personnel to carry out auditing tasks, including the development and installation of audit-related software.

Security auditing is used to accomplish tasks such as:

testing the effectiveness of your security policy

testing for adherence to the security policy

detecting a system compromise

assisting in the analysis of a system attack

gathering evidence to prosecute a system intruder

In order to be most effective, security auditing should be performed on all computers within an organization on a regular basis. The level of auditing performed may vary according to the importance and function of the system under audit. For example, a machine that processes payroll information might be examined more thoroughly than a system used for general data processing. Security auditing functions can be divided into six areas:

7.2.1.1 New System Installation Security Audits Every new computer system installed on your organization's network is a source of potential problems. The purpose of the new system installation audit is to ensure conformance to your organization's new system installation policy. New system security audits should also check for the existence of known security vulnerabilities (e.g., buggy versions of important system programs) and general configuration problems that might lead to a security compromise.

7.2.1.2 Regular Automated Audit Checks Regular security auditing checks can be performed using automated tools, many of which are freely available on the Internet. Regular security audits can reveal a "visitation" by an intruder or illicit activity by insiders. A regular security audit check could also include a check of physical security controls, e.g., "floor checks" to ensure that computer and communication rooms are locked and that system backups are stored properly.

7.2.1.3 Random Security Audit Checks Random security audit checks are usually done to test for conformance to security policies and standards or to check for the existence of a specific class of problems (e.g., the presence of a vulnerability reported by a vendor). When testing for conformance to policies and standards, the security audit should be conducted without notice (or on very short notice) so employees do not have an opportunity to "undo" changes they have made that don't conform to policy. A random security check might be as simple as examining the permission modes of a few files, or it could be as involved as running a comprehensive network-auditing package on an entire network.

7.2.1.4 Nightly Audits of Critical Files Nightly security audits can be used to assess the integrity of critical files (e.g., the password file) or databases (e.g., payroll or sales and marketing information). These audit checks can be performed by programs that are automatically invoked by the system each night. If these special audits involve most of the important system configuration files, they can also serve to help detect intruders and unauthorized insider activities.

7.2.1.5 User Account Activity Audits User account audits focus on detecting dormant and invalid accounts. This function requires the existence of an account management database that contains information about which users have valid accounts on which machines, what their appropriate user IDs and group memberships are, etc. These audits should report invalid user accounts and user accounts that have not been accessed for some period (e.g., 90 or 120 days). Intruders and insiders attempting illicit activities often establish bogus accounts or use dormant accounts to perform their activities.

7.2.1.6 System Log File Auditing and Analysis This type of auditing function was discussed in section 2.3.4. Most multiuser operating systems provide a basic logging facility that, if used to its potential, can help administrators to discover abnormal activities on the system.

7.2.2 Other Ongoing Security Activities Although security audits and audit trail analysis play significant roles in ensuring the ongoing success of your security policy and controls, there are various other tasks that your support staff will need to accomplish. They will need to stay current on new security threats and the new technology used to respond to those threats. This will require them to monitor security newsgroups and mailing lists, to review new material available on the World Wide Web, and to maintain personal contact with other security professionals. Appendix B lists a number of such information resources.

Another important ongoing task is installation of security patches for security-critical software. Many vendors maintain mailing lists to distribute announcements regarding vulnerabilities detected in their software. At least one member of your support staff should subscribe to all appropriate vendor contact mailing lists. Security patch information is also frequently distributed by incident response organizations, such as CERT and CIAC, and by "full-disclosure" security mailing lists. Your technical support staff should document all security patches and fixes that are implemented at your site. You might even consider establishing a policy stating that appropriate security patches must be installed within a specified length of time after their publication.

A final important ongoing security task is to provide security awareness training. Several times throughout this booklet, we have mentioned the importance of training employees, users, and support staff about security policies and procedures. You might consider developing a security Web page local to your organization where your support staff can publish the organization's security policies and procedures, summaries of security incidents at your site, and summaries of recent Internet security advisories and incidents.

Although these ongoing activities may be performed by non-management personnel, management personnel should be aware of and should support the work necessary to keep the organization's security infrastructure current and functional.

Appendix A: The Top Ten Computer Security Problems That Plague Organizations

It has been our experience that many organizations face the same security problems over and over again. We have heard "war stories" from system administrators and security analysts who share their tales of success and failure in battling security problems on a daily basis. Articles in newspapers, high-tech magazines, and Internet newsgroups often mention the same subset of security problems. The good news is that most of these problems can be resolved or greatly reduced with existing software and an appropriate commitment of human resources.

In this section, we provide a rundown of what we and others in the computer security community consider to be the ten most common computer security problems plaguing organizations today. Our goal is to provide you, the manager, with some food for thought when considering how to implement security at your organization.

This "top ten list" also appears on the "1996 Network Security Roadmap" poster distributed by the System Administration, Networking & Security (SANS) Conference Office (electronic mail address: *<sans@clark.net>*).

A.1 Insufficient Site Resources

The most common underlying problem in computer security appears to be that organizations are not dedicating sufficient resources to implement the level of security their organization needs. Although this problem is not as widespread as it was in the early 1990s, we still hear many complaints from system support personnel who claim that computer security at their site is just somebody's "side job." Maintaining proper security requires much more than a side job. We hope that by reading this booklet you are taking the first step toward allocating more resources toward implementing and maintaining security. If your organization does not have enough resources to hire one or more full-time security analysts, then distribute the security development, implementation, and maintenance tasks among enough employees to get the job done.

A.2 Insufficient Support or Authority

The second problem is that network and system support personnel often do not the have management support or the authority to deploy appropriate security measures. Without the proper management backing and authority, system support personnel cannot always implement appropriate security controls and enforce security policy. It is crucial for management to provide support and backing and to be a part of the process of determining what security controls are appropriate for the organization.

A.3 Systems with Security Problems

The third problem is that vendors are still shipping systems with poor default security configurations, and customers are still buying these systems even though they know the systems have security problems. As long as customers are willing to buy software with known programming bugs and security flaws, many vendors will continue to ship such software rather than incur the expense of fixing the problems.

If enough organizations apply pressure, vendors could be motivated to provide better, less flawed software. If the vendors still don't respond, then organizations should not buy products from vendors with poor track records in responding to complaints about security flaws in the systems they sell.

A.4 Unused Vendor Patches

The fourth problem is that customer sites are not installing vendor patches for known security problems. Vendors have greatly improved their patch distribution process since early 1990s. For example, many of the major hardware vendors now have a special electronic mailing list to distribute vulnerability information. Unfortunately, the common problem now is that the patches are not installed by affected organizations, or there is such a long delay between the time the vulnerability is announced and the time the patch is applied that intruders are able to exploit the bug to gain access to unpatched systems.

Management should insist that all appropriate security patches for vendor software be installed in a timely fashion. The installation process should be documented so those who have a need to know can find out which patches have been installed. If necessary, establish a local electronic mailing list to inform the group of people who will need to install the patch, and if necessary, establish a formal policy governing the installation of security patches.

Vendors that do not alert customers to security patches, either directly or through response organizations such as CERT, should be pressured by their customers to implement a notification program. Vendors should also be encouraged to minimize the time between the discovery of a security flaw and the release of a patch to correct it.

A.5 Unencrypted Reusable Passwords

Sites still using a login authentication system that employs reusable passwords transmitted over the network unencrypted is a fifth problem. Clear-text (unencrypted) reusable passwords traversing the Internet have been known security problems for many years. Password sniffing attacks have become a favored intruder technique in the 1990s. Solutions to this problem include one-time passwords and tokens, discussed in sections 2.2.4 and 2.2.5. Another solution is the use of network authentication packages such as Kerberos, discussed in section 2.4.2.

A.6 Poor Dialup Security Measures

The sixth problem is that sites do not implement good dialup security measures. The issue of remote access is still a major problem for some sites. Many organization still rely on modem pools, terminal servers, and dial-back modems that have no proper security controls. Intruders often use these systems as stepping-stones to an attack on that site or other sites.

Many companies resolve this problem by using a single point of entrance into the company network (e.g., a firewall) and by forcing users to authenticate themselves using a hardware token. There has been significant growth in the market for remote access systems, so the issue of secure remote access is likely to remain a hot topic for the foreseeable future.

A.7 Open Network Access

Sites not monitoring or restricting network access to their internal hosts is a seventh problem. Unrestricted and unmonitored network access to your internal systems can be a major source of problems. Anyone on the Internet can launch an attack or scan your internal network for possible vulnerabilities. Even if you decide not to use a firewall to filter network traffic passing between the Internet and your site, there are software tools that can be used on particularly sensitive machines to filter and monitor network traffic. Using such a tool will at least reduce your risk. Such software is available freely on the Internet and from commercial vendors.

A.8 Inconsistently Installed User Accounts

Inconsistent installation of new user accounts, the eighth problem, may result in easily exploited accounts. Some organizations still create all new user accounts with the same default password or with a password that is derived from username information. A related problem is that some vendors ship operating systems with default support accounts that have no passwords or that have the same passwords on all systems shipped by that vendor.

The inconsistent account installation problem can be reduced or resolved by implementing an account management procedure that defines the method used to install accounts, the permissions to be used on user directories and environment configuration files, and the algorithm used to generate a user's initial password.

A.9 Poor Account Monitoring and Expiration

A ninth problem is that sites often do not monitor account activity, and they do not always remove the accounts of terminated users. Many sites have no established policy regarding removal of user accounts after employees leave. These dormant accounts are often discovered and used by intruders or malicious employees. A user account should be disabled and removed after the account's owner leaves the organization. If other employees need to access files stored in that account, those files should be moved to another location (e.g., into the directories of the employees who need to access the files).

Although establishing a policy about removal of user accounts can help this problem from a management standpoint, use of an account management package can help to solve the problem technically. At a large site with thousands of machines and users, it can be nearly impossible to determine on which machines a departed employee had accounts. A centralized account database managed by an account management package can reduce the administrative workload of dealing with account creation and deletion. Most UNIX variants shipped with modern systems include at least some rudimentary centralized account management software.

A.10 Poorly Configured and Audited New Systems

Finally, sites may not implement and enforce procedures and standards for installing new host machines on their network. Rogue and misconfigured hosts on a network are easy prey for intruders. Especially, if your organization has an open network (no firewall protection), every system installed on the network should meet some sort of minimum security standards and should be audited on a regular basis. Otherwise, these "untouched" systems can become a source of hidden vulnerabilities that may eventually be exploited by an intruder.

Various security checklists and automated software packages are available on the Internet to help administrators configure and properly audit newly installed systems.

Appendix B: Useful Computer Security Resources

The field of computer security is characterized by constant change. New security vulnerabilities are constantly discovered, and patches to correct those vulnerabilities are frequently released. Increasingly, hardware and software products that eliminate whole classes of security vulnerabilities are being developed. Only by staying up to date with the latest computer security developments can you and your organization hope to keep your information systems secure.

When it comes to computer security resources, there's good news and bad news. The good news is that the most valuable resources are available completely free of charge on the Internet. The bad news is the volume of information available—a person could spend 24 hours per day, 7 days per week monitoring the various sources of computer security news and still miss some information. In this appendix, we present those computer security resources that we feel are both of high quality and relevant to managers. We feel that these resources offer the highest ratio of valuable information provided to time investment required.

B.1 Organizations

B.1.1 Government Organizations
The National Computer Security Center (NCSC) administers the Trusted Product Evaluation Program (see section 6.3), which evaluates products according to the Orange Book guidelines. The NCSC can be contacted at

> National Computer Security Center
> 9800 Savage Road
> Fort George G. Meade, MD 20755-6000

The National Institute of Standards and Technology (NIST) Information Technology Laboratory (ITL) develops standards and procedures related to computer systems security. The organization also offers services to help educate the public about computer security. The ITL is composed of what used to be the Computer Systems Laboratory

(CSL) and the Computing and Applied Mathematics Laboratory (CAML). NIST's Web page can be found at *<http://www.nist.gov/>*, and the ITL Web page can be found at *<http://www.nist.gov/itl/>*.

The US Department of Energy Computer Incident Advisory Capability (CIAC) provides services related to computer security for Department of Energy contractors and employees, but much of its information, including security alerts, is available to the public. The CIAC Web page can be found at< *http://ciac.llnl.gov/>*.CIAC can be contacted by email at<*ciac@llnl.gov>* or by telephone at (510) 422-8193.

B.1.2 Non-Governmental Organizations

B.1.2.1 CERT The Computer Emergency Response Team (CERT) was started in November 1988 by the government's Advanced Research Projects Agency (ARPA) as a response to the Internet worm incident. It is currently part of the Software Engineering Institute (SEI), a federal research and development center funded by the Department of Defense and operated by Carnegie Mellon University. CERT attempts to serve as a "reliable, trusted, 24-hour, single point of contact for [computer security] emergencies." The organization collects incident reports from organizations that have experienced computer security problems and attempts to help those organizations repair their security infrastructure. CERT also issues periodic advisories to the Internet community regarding both specific security vulnerabilities and general trends in security attacks. Additionally, CERT redistributes security bulletins issued by vendors and offers various workshops and seminars. The CERT Web page is located at *<http://www.cert.org/>*. The CERT Coordination Center can be contacted by email at *<cert@cert.org>* or by telephone at (412) 268-7090.

B.1.2.2 FIRST Forum of Incident Response and Security Teams (FIRST) is a coalition of computer security incident response teams from government, industry, and education. FIRST's goal is to "foster cooperation and coordination in incident prevention, to prompt rapid reaction to incidents, and to promote information sharing among members and the community at large." The FIRST Web page can be found at *<http://www.first.org/>*. FIRST can be contacted by email at *<first-sec@first.org>* or by telephone at (310) 975-3359.

B.1.3 Companies
Many computer system and software vendors offer security information related to their products. We list the email addresses for reporting security problems to a number of vendors, as well as the address for each vendor's main home page. Additional information can be found in the computer security vendor contacts FAQ at *<ftp://ftp.iss.net/pub/faq/vendor>*.

Cray Research	*<support@cray.com>*
	<http://www.cray.com/>
HP	*<security-alert@hp.com>*
	<http://www.hp.com/>
IBM	*<services@austin.ibm.com>*
	<http://www.ibm.com/>
Motorola	*<security-alert@mdc.mot.com>*
	<http://www.mot.com>
NeXT	*<ask_next@next.com>*
	<http://www.next.com/>
Novell	*<1-800-4-UNIVEL>*
	<http://www.novel.com/>
SGI	*<security-alert@sgi.com>*
	<http://www.sgi.com/>
Sun	*<security-alert@sun.com>*
	<http://www.sun.com/>

B.2 Mailing lists

Mailing lists related to computer security abound. Most are technical in nature, dealing with specific security flaws in operating systems and application programs. A few are of a more general nature, and we list them here. A comprehensive list of security mailing lists is maintained by Christopher Klaus *<cklaus@iss.net>* of Internet Security Systems. The list is available by sending an electronic mail message with the body "send index" to *<info@iss.net>*. The document is also available by anonymous FTP from *<ftp://ftp.iss.net/pub/faq/maillist>*. The list we provide is based in part on that list.

Some mailing lists are "moderated"; others are "unmoderated." Unmoderated lists allow one person to send a message to the entire list directly. Moderated lists require that a submitted message be approved by the moderator before it is distributed to the list members. As a result, moderated lists generally have a higher "signal-to-noise ratio" than unmoderated lists. But unmoderated lists are far more plentiful than moderated lists because they do not require anyone to serve in the time-consuming role of moderator.

B.2.1 Academic Firewalls

This unmoderated list carries discussion of firewalls and other security issues as they relate to academic institutions. To subscribe, send the message "subscribe academic-firewalls" to <*majordomo@net.tamu.edu*>.

B.2.2 Alert

This low-traffic, moderated list carries various security tidbits, some relating to the list's sponsoring organization, Internet Security Systems. To join, send a message with the text "subscribe alert" to <*request-alert@iss.net*>.

B.2.3 Best of Security

This unmoderated list carries information about security vulnerabilities, particularly those related to UNIX systems. Although fairly technical, it is not as technical as most of the other technically oriented security lists. To join, send a message with the text "sub-scribe best-of-security" to <*majordomo@suburbia.net*>.

B.2.4 CERT-ADVISORY

This mailing list is used by CERT (see section B.1.2.1) to distribute announcements of security vulnerabilities. To join, send a message to <*cert-advisory-request@cert.org*> with your email address.

B.2.5 CERT-TOOLS

This mailing list occasionally carries announcements of security-related tools. It is run by CERT. To join, send email to <*cert-tools-request@cert.org*> with your email address.

B.2.6 CIAC-BULLETIN

This mailing list is used by CIAC (see section B.1.1) to distribute announcements of security vulnerabilities. To join, send the message "subscribe CIAC-BULLETIN (your last name), (your first name), (your phone number)" to <*ciac-listproc@llnl.gov*>.

B.2.7 CIAC-NOTES

This mailing list is used by CIAC to distribute non-urgent information related to computer security. To join, send the message "subscribe CIAC-NOTES (your last name), (your first name), (your phone number)" to <*ciac-lisproc@llnl.gov*>.

B.2.8 Firewalls

This unmoderated list carries discussions related to network firewalls. To join, send the message "subscribe firewalls" to <*majordomo@greatcircle.com*>.

B.2.9 INFSEC-L

The Information Systems Security Forum is an unmoderated list carrying discussions related to information system security. To subscribe, send "sub infsec-l (your name)" to <*listserv@etsuadmn.etsu.edu*>.

B.2.10 Intrusion Detection Systems

To join, send "subscribe ids" to *<majordomo@uow.edu.au>*.

B.2.11 Legal Aspects of Computer Crime

To join, send "subscribe lacc" to *<majordomo@suburbia.net>*.

B.2.12 RISKS

One of the oldest security-related mailing lists, RISKS deals with the entire range of risks posed by computer systems. The list is moderated. To subscribe, send "subscribe" to *<risks-request@csl.sri.com>*. The list can also be read as a USENET newsgroup, *<comp.risks>*.

B.2.13 UNINFSEC (University Information Security Forum)

This unmoderated list carries discussion related to information security within the context of educational institutions. To subscribe, send the message "subscribe uninfsec" to *<listserv@cuvmc.ais.columbia.edu>*.

B.2.14 VIRUS-L

This moderated list carries discussion related to computer viruses. To subscribe, send the message "subscribe virus-l (your name)" to *<LISTSERV@lehigh.edu>*.

B.2.15 Virus Alert

This moderated list carries "urgent virus warnings." To subscribe, send the message "subscribe valert-l (your name)" to *<LISTSERV@lehigh.edu>*. Note that all messages distributed to Virus Alert are also distributed to the VIRUS-L list (but not vice versa).

B.3. Web Pages

The following Web pages contain pointers to useful security resources.

<http://www.cs.purdue.edu/homes/spaf/hotlists/csec-top.html>
<http://ciac.llnl.gov>
<http://csrc.ncsl.nist.gov/first/>
<http://www.alw.nih.gov/Security/security.html>
<http://www.auscert.org.au>
<http://www.cert.dfn.de/eng >
<http://www.cs.purdue.edu/coast/coast.html >
<http://www.sware.com/>
<http://www.telstra.com.au/info/security.html>
<http://www.yahoo.com/Business_and_Economy/Companies/Computers/Security/>
<http://www.crpht.lu/CNS/html/PubServ/Security/security-home.html>

B.4 USENET Newsgroups

The following newsgroups carry discussion of computer security issues.

<comp.security.announce>—A moderated newsgroup carrying urgent computer security announcements

<comp.security.unix>—An unmoderated newsgroup carrying discussion related to the security of UNIX systems.

<comp.lang.java.security>— An unmoderated newsgroup carrying discussion related to security issues pertaining to the Java programming language

<comp.security.firewalls>—An unmoderated newsgroup carrying discussion related to computer network firewalls

<comp.security.misc >—An unmoderated newsgroup carrying miscellaneous security discussions

<comp.os.netware.security>—An unmoderated newsgroup carrying discussion of security issues related to Novell's NetWare product

<comp.risks>—A moderated newsgroup that mirrors the RISKS mailing list (see section B.2.12)

<comp.virus>—A moderated newsgroup that mirrors the VIRUS-L mailing list (see section B.2.14)

<comp.admin.policy>—An unmoderated newsgroup that carries general discussion about computer policies

<alt.security.pgp>—An unmoderated newsgroup carrying discussion of the PGP system (see section 2.3.3.2)

<alt.security>—An unmoderated newsgroup carrying discussion of security matters

B.5 Books

Chapman, D. Brent, and Zwicky, Elizabeth. *Building Internet Firewalls.* Sebastopol, CA: O'Reilly & Associates, 1995.

Cheswick, William, and Bellovin, Steven. *Firewalls and Internet Security: Repelling the Wily Hacker.* Reading, MA: Addison Wesley Longman, 1994.

Farrow, Rik. *UNIX® System Security.* Reading, MA: Addison Wesley Longman, 1991.

Ford, Warwick. *Computer Communications Security: Principles, Standard Protocols and Techniques.* Upper Saddle River, NJ: Prentice Hall PTR, 1994.

Garfinkel, Simson. *PGP: Pretty Good Privacy.* Sebastopol, CA: O'Reilly & Associates, 1994.

Garfinkel, Simson, and Spafford, Gene. *Practical UNIX & Internet Security.* 2d ed. Sebastopol, CA: O'Reilly & Associates, 1996.

Icove, David; Seger, Karl; and VonStorch, William. *Computer Crime: A Crimefighter's Handbook.* Sebastopol, CA: O'Reilly & Associates, 1995.

Russell, Deborah, and Gangemi, G.T., Sr. *Computer Security Basics.* Sebastopol, CA: O'Reilly & Associates, 1991.

Stoll, Clifford. *The Cuckoo's Egg.* New York: Doubleday, 1989.